Doña Gracia
of the
House of Nasi

SOME OTHER BOOKS BY THE SAME AUTHOR

THE LAST FLORENTINE REPUBLIC, 1925

THE CASALE PILGRIM, 1929

HISTORY OF THE JEWS IN VENICE, 1930

A JEWISH BOOK OF DAYS, 1931

A HISTORY OF THE MARRANOS, 1932

THE NEPHEW OF THE ALMIGHTY, 1933

A LIFE OF MENASSEH BEN ISRAEL, 1934

A BIRD'S-EYE VIEW OF JEWISH HISTORY, 1935

THE RITUAL MURDER LIBEL AND THE JEW, 1935

THE JEWISH CONTRIBUTION TO CIVILIZATION, 1938

ANGLO-JEWISH LETTERS, 1938

THE MAGNIFICENT ROTHSCHILDS, 1939

THE SASSOON DYNASTY, 1941

A HISTORY OF THE JEWS IN ENGLAND, 1941

THE HISTORY OF THE JEWS IN ITALY, 1946

GRACIA MENDES, THE YOUNGER
ABOUT 1553
medal made by Pastorius de' Pastorini in Ferrara

Doña Gracia
of the
House of Nasi

CECIL ROTH

The Jewish Publication Society of America
PHILADELPHIA   1977/5738

TO THE MEMORY OF

HENRIETTA SZOLD

TABLE OF CONTENTS

LIST OF ILLUSTRATIONS

PREFACE

THE GENESIS of this book must be explained. A short time ago, I was invited to write a biography of that extraordinarily romantic figure of Jewish history, Joseph Nasi, Duke of Naxos. Though the idea had never before entered my head, it fascinated me and the work proceeded with a rapidity which I found almost disconcerting. But, as the book began to take shape, it divided itself naturally into two sections. In the first, the predominant interest was not the Duke himself but his aunt, Doña Gracia, formerly Beatrice de Luna, mother of the Duchess — his model, his first patroness and his constant inspiration. Gradually, her figure began to detach itself from the background and her features became clearer to me. I realized in the end that she was of importance in Jewish history, not as the harbinger of her nephew, but on her own account. Her adventurous career in her younger days, her heroic work to thwart the Inquisition and organize the flight of the Marranos from the Peninsula, the great part that she played in public and communal affairs, first in the Low Countries, then in Italy, then in Turkey, her masculine reactions whenever a report of persecution in any part of the world reached her ears, her single-minded leadership at the time of the holocaust at Ancona in 1556 mark her off as one of the outstanding figures of Jewish history, not of her own day alone, but of all time. What her nephew did during her life was almost entirely due to her inspiration and tutelage: it was only after her death that his own personality developed to the full.

In view of this, it has seemed preferable to divide my work into two parts and to publish the life of Doña Gracia Nasi as an independent volume. This is all the more desirable, it seems to me, in view of the fact that, the rôle of the Jewish woman in history having been essentially domestic (though not for that reason any less important), there were until the past generation very few outstanding Jewesses who could form the subject of biography. Doña Gracia is one of the sparse exceptions, and it would be regrettable for this opportunity to be lost.

The sixteenth century was, in fact, the age of famous women — Elizabeth, Mary, and Mary Queen of Scots in Great Britain; Lucrezia Borgia, Isabella d'Este, Caterina Sforza, Vittoria Colonna and a score of others in Italy, Catherine de' Medicis in France, and many more. It is noteworthy that Gracia Nasi belonged to the same age. But she did not stand alone in the Jewish world at this time: it was the age too of Benvenida Abrabanel in Ferrara and of Esther Kyra in Constantinople — to cite the names of two only who were active in public life. I have gone out of my way to speak of these also at some length, for it is a remarkable illustration of the fashion in which currents in general life are reflected in that of the Jewish community. There is indeed one outstanding difference. The women who attained eminence in European history at this time tended to be not merely famous, but also notorious — a quality or rather characteristic which (it may be said) these Jewish heroines generally lacked. In depicting the background, I have wherever possible allowed the contemporary observers to speak in their own inimitable, racy style.

This book will be followed shortly by another, which will deal with the amazing career of the Duke of Naxos. But while the sequel will be incomprehensible without a knowledge of the first half of the story, this volume is complete and self-contained.

I must add in conclusion that any parallels with the conditions of our own day, which may be noticed in this work, are due to the irony of history and not the imagination of the author.

CECIL ROTH

Oxford, December, 1946.

Atlantic
Ocean

North
Sea

IRELAND

ENGLAND

London

Antwerp

Aix la Chapelle

Seine R.

Nantes

Paris

FRANCE

Bern

SWIS...

Bay of
Biscay

FR. COMTE

Bordeaux

Lyons

SAVOY

Rhone R.

Avignon

NAVARRE

Marseilles

Gen...

PORTUGAL

Ebro R.

Saragossa

Madrid

CORSICA

SPAIN

BALEARIC IS.

SARDINIA

Lisbon

Mediterranean

Tangier

Oran

Algiers

A F R I C A

Sus...

Scale of Miles

0   100   200   300   400   500

W. Streckfuss

Doña Gracia
of the
House of Nasi

CHAPTER I

The House of Mendes

Boys played cheerful music at the head of the interminable processions, as they toiled their way westward under the broiling midsummer sun; so the rabbis had bidden, in order to maintain the broken spirits of their people. For this was the crowning disaster.

Over a period of at least fifteen centuries Jews had lived in Spain, where they had attained the greatest height of achievement that the Diaspora in Europe had known. The service of the Synagogue was raised to a higher plane by the inspired poetry of the Castilian Jehudah ha-Levi and his compeers; every Jewish scholar conned the legal handbooks of Isaac al-Fasi of Lucena and Jacob ben Asher of Toledo; the Church itself had unwittingly adopted the writings of Solomon ibn Gabirol of Malaga, imagining him to be a Mozarebe, and Christian philosophers venerated the acumen if not the conclusions of Moses ben Maimon of Cordova. Spanish Jewry had achieved high distinction too in secular life. No court of the Peninsula, Christian or Moorish, failed to employ at one time or another the services of Jewish counsellors, diplomats and financiers; Jewish savants of the time of Alfonso the Wise had assisted in moulding Castilian as a literary medium; Jewish astronomers had prepared the way for the discoveries of Columbus; even the fate-fraught marriage between Ferdinand and Isabella, not many years before, had been brought about largely through the foresight and adroitness of Abraham Senior, the financier-magnate who enjoyed the titular dignity of Chief Rabbi, or *Rab de la Corte*, of Castile.

All this now belonged to history, and there was no hope of renewal. Spain had expressed its traditional religious zeal and its newly-found political unity by expelling the last Moslem ruler of Granada by force of arms. Inevitably, this was followed by an onslaught upon the remaining religious minority, the Jews, who were suspected moreover of consciously and deliberately maintaining the loyalties of those converted coreligionists of theirs, styled "New Christians," who for the past century — since the great outbreak of violence at Seville on Ash Wednesday, 1391 — had been so numerous in the country from end to end. In the captured Alhambra, still scented with the perfumes of its former Moorish masters, the Catholic sovereigns signed, on March 31, 1492, the pitiless Edict of Expulsion which was intended to end the Jewish connection with Spain for all time. Within four months, all professing Jews were to leave the country.

Now, as the time limit neared, all the roads leading to the coast or to the frontiers were choked with refugees. They had abandoned their lovely synagogues, henceforth to be converted into churches or stables. They had left the ancient cemeteries, where the remains of their ancestors rested, in the hands of the Christian neighbors, making arrangements where possible for their upkeep "in perpetuity." They had disposed of all their property at ridiculous prices. With them, they could take away only one treasure — the *Sifre Torah*, the scrolls of the

Law given at Sinai, which the graybeards hugged to their bosoms as they faltered along the dusty highways.

A contemporary Spanish observer, no sympathizer with the Jews, described the pitiful odyssey in agonizing terms. The exiles had to pass the night, more often than not, in the fields. Some fell out on the way from fatigue, some from sickness; old men died, children were born, under the open skies, far from the nearest township and sometimes remote from help. Some of the Christians who witnessed the scene were filled with a warped compassion and, mingling with the exiles as they plodded past, begged them to submit to baptism — but in vain, for a rabbi or scholar was at hand straightway to encourage the weary and despairing. When the columns began to move, the women sang their plaintive oriental melodies, while the children played their tambours and trumpets, as they had been bidden. As they came in sight of the sea which marked the limit of their beloved Spain and the beginning of the anguish of exile, the victims could be seen to weep and to tear their hair and to call upon the Almighty to favor them too by a miracle as He had their fathers at the time of the Exodus from Egypt, by bringing them across dryshod. The waters remained undivided. But those who came to Seville might have seen in the harbor at Palos a group of caravels waiting to hoist sail. It was Christopher Columbus' tiny fleet on the eve of the most momentous sea-voyage in history.

The greatest single body of exiles unenterprisingly crossed the frontier into Portugal, the only neighboring land which was open to them, not suspecting what further tribulations awaited them there. All who so wished were permitted to enter the country on the payment of

a poll-tax of eight *cruzados* for each adult, it being stipulated that they would not remain longer than eight
months: within this period, the king promised to find
shipping for their transport whithersoever they desired.
The number of those who availed themselves of the
terms of this agreement is reckoned to have amounted
to nearly one hundred thousand souls. In addition to
these ordinary immigrants and to a number of craftsmen
who were admitted almost without formality because of
their potential importance in the national economy
(especially in time of war), thirty prominent families from
Castile were permitted to establish themselves in Oporto,
where they henceforth played a foremost role in many
branches of activity. (Their descendants were to include
the luckless philosopher Uriel Acosta.) Another six hundred wealthy householders, who could afford to pay a
poll-tax of one hundred *cruzados* apiece, were allowed to
settle at will in other parts of the country, where they
tried — as so many other persons belonging to their
stock have been compelled to do, in similar circumstances,
throughout the ages — to piece together their shattered
lives again. Included in their number were members of
all of the most important families in Spanish Jewish history. The amazing story of some of their descendants
will be recounted in this work; the vicissitudes of the
group as a whole — one of the most tragic and most
heroic episodes in human annals — will constitute a good
part of the background.[1]

For the first few years, the condition of the exiles of
the upper class at least was relatively favorable, the
atmosphere improving indeed in some respects with the
accession of King Manoel the Fortunate to the throne

in 1495. The story of how conditions changed is sordid to a degree. Ferdinand and Isabella, like their counterparts in our own day, considered antisemitism to be a commodity for export and used every possible means, diplomatic and otherwise, to hunt down the miserable refugees whom they had already ruined and uprooted. That some were installed in Portugal, almost on their own frontier, appeared to them a perpetual personal affront. But they had in their hands (it seemed an act of Providence) a lever which could help them to secure their object. Their daughter Isabella was one of the most desirable matches in Europe — especially for the young King Manoel, since, if they were married, there was a prospect that his posterity would ultimately rule over the whole of the Peninsula, conferring political unity upon it at last. Neither the parents nor their yet-more-fanatical daughter would, however, consent to the union unless the smaller country was "purified" of Jews as the larger one had been. As is always the case, political advantage outweighed every other consideration. On the last day but one of November, 1496, the marriage treaty was signed. Less than a week later a royal decree was issued at Muje banishing all Jews (as well as Moslems) from Portugal within ten months.

The ink was scarcely dry upon this document, when Manoel began to consider the warnings of the wiser members of his Council of State that the expulsion of this diligent and thrifty section of the population would weaken the country and strengthen its enemies in Africa and elsewhere. There was only one way by which the two alternatives, of political caution on the one hand and religious zeal on the other, could be reconciled. If the

Jews could be brought over to Christianity *en masse* he
would have achieved simultaneously the supreme triumphs of saving their souls and benefitting the country
by absorbing their ability — a consummation for which
many in various lands of Europe had hoped, but no one
had hitherto attained.

All his energies in the next few months were devoted
to this object. First, with shrewd psychological insight
(it is said that a renegade advised him in this), he struck
at the parents through the children. On March 19, 1497,
orders were issued for all those between the ages of four
and fourteen years to be presented for baptism on the
following Sunday — the first day of the feast of Passover
according to the Jewish calendar — and thereafter to be
brought up as Christians, remote from their parents'
care. Scenes of indescribable horror were witnessed all
over the country that day, some fathers strangling their
sons in a last embrace rather than surrender them to a
fate that they considered worse than death; yet only in
ridiculously few cases was there the desired effect of making them accompany their progeny into apostasy, in the
hope that they might keep together. Sometimes the age
limit was disregarded, and the process of enforced baptism was indiscriminate. More than thirty years later,
the aged Bishop Coutinho still remembered with horror
episodes he had witnessed with his own eyes at this tragic
time, when more than once he saw a heartbroken father
bring his son to the font, protesting and calling God to
witness that they wished to die together in the Law of
Moses.

The main problem remained: and the final date fixed
for the departure of the Jews from the country was now

imminent. Some 20,000 of them, from all parts of the country, had assembled by the king's order at Lisbon — the only port whence embarkation was ultimately allowed. Here, they were cooped up in vast numbers without food or drink in the hope that their privations would open their eyes to the true faith. Periodicals visits were paid to them by renegades and friars, who had the mission of persuading them that life was worth a Mass. Many, their powers of resistance at an end, succumbed to the temptation at last. Those who still refused were kept closely guarded until the time limit for their departure had lapsed. They were then informed that the penalty for their disobedience was enslavement and that they could recover their liberty only by adopting the dominant faith. Some were now dragged to the font by brute force. The rest, still protesting, had Holy Water flung over them from a distance and were declared to be Christians. It was only the barest handful who were ultimately transported to Africa — the remnant of the ancient and once renowned Portuguese Jewry. The vast majority (and they included most of the better-class exiles from Spain of five years previous) were now titular Christians — the learned and the unlearned, the rich and the poor, the merchants, the rabbis, the teachers, the craftsmen, the mendicants, the wastrels, the saints, all alike.[2]

In place of their former Jewish names, they were now known by the appellations — sometimes nobiliary — of those who had stood their sponsors at baptism. But it made no difference to their beliefs, and at heart they were still Jews, conforming as much as possible to their old faith and as little as possible to the new — "Marranos," as the Spanish and Portuguese called them, from an old term of opprobrium originally meaning "pig." It would have been ludicrous at this stage to punish them drastically for minor ritual lapses, yet any demonstration of Jewish allegiance or sympathy was nevertheless highly dangerous henceforth, as was shown by occasional prosecutions and more than one murderous attack.

Among the victims of the forced conversion there were certain members of the ancient house of Benveniste.[3] This was one of the oldest and most distinguished in the history of Spanish Jewry. An Isaac Benveniste (the name probably means "the welcome") had been body-physician to the kings of Aragon in the twelfth century and had been recognized by his coreligionists as their "prince," transmitting this title to his son, Sheshet, after him; in the fourteenth century Joseph Benveniste had been counsellor to Alphonso XI of Castile; while in the fifteenth, Abraham Benveniste had put the finances of the kingdom of Aragon in order and had enjoyed the rank of Crown Rabbi. This eminent and pious leader of his people had died about 1452; and possibly it was one of his immediate descendants who was living in Spain at the time of the tragic events of forty years later, when he migrated into Portugal with his two young sons, Semah and Meir.[4] As Christians, the latter adopted the name of Mendes, being known henceforth as Francisco and Diogo Mendes respectively. There is some reason to believe that the father, perhaps baptized under different auspices, was known now as Henrique Nuñes.[5]

It is probable that the family was well-to-do from the outset, belonging to the six hundred privileged families from Spain who had been benevolently received in 1492. In any case, as Christians they found open before them dazzling avenues of profit which would have been closed to them as Jews. It was the golden age of Portuguese history. Not long since, Vasco da Gama — advised by Jewish scholars, aided by Jewish enterprise and using maps and instruments of Jewish manufacture — had discovered the sea-route to India round the Cape of Good Hope. Now all the spices, gems and luxuries of the Far East, formerly imported by way of the Red Sea, Egypt and Venice, found their main European outlet on the shores of the Tagus, with the result that within a few years the Portuguese revenues were increased fourfold. New opportunities now presented themselves to alert businessmen in connection with the distribution of these commodities in the great untapped markets of northern Europe. The brothers Mendes, originally, it seems, dealers in precious stones, took an outstanding part in this, so that before the sixteenth century was far advanced they had attained an important position in the commercial world of Lisbon.

Historians speak of the Mendes "banking-house." But we should not be misled by the name. Banking in the modern sense did not yet exist. A firm such as this would have been primarily interested in the acquisition and sale of precious commodities from overseas and the transmission of payments. It might, however, prefer to reinvest its profits locally, thus extending its interests. At the same time, it might place at the disposal of its clients (who were thereby saved the risk and expense of conveying bullion) the mechanism it had elaborated for the transmission of money from country to country, arranging for bills of exchange at rates of profit which, at their smallest, would today be considered preposterous. De-

posit banking was as yet hardly known, though money
might be accepted by the firm for safe custody or for use
in trade on lucrative terms; while, on the other hand, it
might be resorted to for private or government loans.
All this, however, would naturally have been subsidiary
to the commercial operations which were the principal
interest of such establishments as this. This was presumably the nature of the business of the Mendes "banking-house" of which so much is read in the records of the
time.

The ex-Jews always married among themselves as far
as possible, so as to ensure the preservation of their
ancestral loyalties from generation to generation. The
elder Mendes brother, Francisco, chose as his wife the
sister of the royal physician, Dr. Miguez.[6] She was
known to the outside world as Beatrice de Luna. (It is to
be noted that at this time surnames were very fluid in
Spain and Portugal, so that members of the same family
often had different appellations; this may perhaps have
been that of her mother's family). In the privacy of her
home she was, however, called Gracia — the equivalent
of the Hebrew, *Hannah* — Nasi. She too belonged to an
ancient and memorable Jewish clan, perhaps allied long
before to that of Beneveniste.

Since the early Middle Ages, there had come into
prominence, here and there in the Diaspora, Jewish leaders or families who had attained a dominating position
among their coreligionists and were considered, in this
or that city or province, to be their official representatives
vis à vis the government, which in its turn sometimes
recognized their position officially. Such a Jewish leader
was termed, in imitation of the "patriarchs" who had

stood at the head of Palestinian Jewry between the second and the fifth centuries, the *Nasi* or Prince. We encounter persons bearing this title in Rome, Narbonne, Sicily, Egypt and elsewhere. In Spain the office seems to have been traditionally associated especially with the community of Barcelona. We know of a Jewish *Nasi* here in the eleventh century in the person of Rabbi Solomon and his son Sheshet, known as Perfect, to be succeeded a century later by the *Nasi* Isaac Beneveniste referred to above and his son Sheshet — physician, bailiff and adviser of successive Aragonese rulers — and by the philosopher Abraham bar Hayya.[7] Later on, in the fifteenth century (by which time the title had presumably become a surname), we find Don Joseph *el Naci* of Medina del Pomar farming the taxes in the kingdom of Castile in 1430, and a namesake (perhaps his grandson) similarly engaged at Briviesca fifty years later.[8] Nothing is known about the latter's career or of his end, but it may well be that he joined the ranks of the exiles in 1492 — perhaps one of the six hundred well-to-do householders who went from Castile into Portugal, where his family continued to live very probably as titular Christians after the tragic events of 1497.

It was in any case from a branch of the great family of Nasi, which had adopted the name of Miguez, that Beatrice de Luna was descended. When in 1528 she became the bride of Francisco Mendes, she was probably about eighteen years of age. We know nothing of her earlier life. It is not ascertainable even whether De Luna was an original Jewish or an acquired Gentile patronymic. (Both are possible, for Jews bearing the name are encountered at more than one place in Spain before the

Expulsion; it was indeed not uncommon subsequently among the Portuguese Marranos, being originally borne by the eminent seventeenth-century practitioner and polemist, Elijah Montalto, physician to Marie de Médicis, Queen of France). It is certain only that her progenitors must have been endowed with exceptionally strong religious feelings, for her own Hebrew loyalties could not have been more passionate. Of obvious beauty, exceptional ability and, above all, remarkable force of character, she combined inherited acumen with a woman's tenderness and an inexhaustible depth of Jewish sympathy. There was, however, nothing as yet to suggest that she was one of the outstanding women in an age peculiarly rich in great female characters — perhaps the most noteworthy Jewess in all history.[9]

In 1536, some eight years after her marriage, Francisco Mendes died, relatively young notwithstanding the great position he had attained in the world of affairs. His widow was left with an infant daughter, probably baptized as Brianda, after one of her mother's sisters, but privately called Reyna ("Queen") — a popular name for Jewesses at this time.[10] In accordance with the terms of the father's will, the administration of his vast fortune was now divided between Beatrice, who was to act in the name of her daughter, and his brother and partner, Diogo, whom he had sent some time earlier to open a branch establishment at Antwerp, and who was already a prominent figure in the commercial life of that place.

The year of Francisco Mendes' death was a dark one for the "New Christians" of Portugal, as the recent converts from Judaism were officially termed. Since the beginning of the century, their condition had steadily

deteriorated and, in 1506, owing to the untimely scepti-
cism of one of them when he was told of a trivial "miracle," there had been a terrible riot against them in Lisbon,
which cost the lives of hundreds of victims. As early as
1515, the king had applied to Rome for the introduction
of the Inquisition into the Portuguese dominions to take
proceedings against the secret Judaizers in the same
manner as was done in Spain. Thanks to constant vigilance, adroit negotiations, and an undending stream of
well-placed gifts, the New Christians had succeeded in
procuring postponement after postponement, but the
fatal hour was now drawing near. A papal Brief of
May 23, 1536, ordered the establishment in the kingdom
of a Holy Office of the Inquisition on the Spanish model.
The New Christians made frenzied efforts to counteract
it and, in fact, managed to secure a succession of reprieves,
but their interlude of tranquility was now nearly over.
No one knew when proceedings might not open and the
skies begin to be polluted by the smoke of the *quemadero*
and the stench of burning flesh.

Life in Lisbon was thus increasingly hazardous for
those who remained secretly attached to their Jewish
heritage. Nor was emigration to a place of freedom easy,
for they were forbidden to transfer themselves to a non-
Christian land, where it was assumed that they would
revert forthwith to their ancestral faith. Travel to northern Europe, luckily, was possible, and many Marranos
took advantage of the opportunity to settle in Antwerp,
with the intention of transferring themselves ultimately
by the devious overland route to Turkey. Antwerp,
moreover, with the great banking-house under Diogo's
direction now at the height of its reputation, held out

natural attractions for Doña Beatrice. Thither therefore
the young widow now betook herself with her infant
daughter, her unmarried sister Brianda, and her nephews,
João Miguez and his young brother, sons of the court
physician.

On their journey, their coffers filled with the accumulated treasure of the defunct Lisbon house, the party
disembarked for a while in England. Here, there was, at
this time, a little colony of Portuguese Marranos, notwithstanding the fact that the Jews were nominally
excluded from the country. We nevertheless know nothing of their life here or of how long they stayed, though
the visit is referred to as being one "of some duration."[11]
Probably it lasted only while enquiries were made in the
Low Countries, through the medium of the local agents
of the House of Mendes, as to whether it would be safe
for them to continue their journey. (This was the usual
procedure at the time, owing to Diogo's tireless interest,
as will be told). In any case, before long they were settled
in Antwerp, the commercial capital of northern Europe.

ADDITIONAL NOTE TO CHAPTER I

THE MENDES-NASI CONNECTION

The account of the Mendes-Nasi family connection given in these pages differs from that in previous monographs and in all current works of reference. It has invariably been stated hitherto that João Miguez, *alias* Joseph Nasi (the later Duke of Naxos), was the son of one of the brothers of Francisco and Diogo Mendes. (His father's Christian name has even been suggested, though with considerable variation — "Gonsalo" in I. Prins' *De Vestiging der Marranen in Noord-Nederland*, p. 41 n., and "Miguel" in Bato's romanticized Hebrew biography). So far as I have been able to find there is no authority for this. The contemporary sources, indeed, inform us that Joseph Nasi was the nephew of Gracia Nasi (Beatrice Mendes); but the assumption that he was the son of her husband's brother is gratuitous. The hypothesis is, moreover, rendered improbable: 1. by the difference of name and 2. by the fact that neither in Diogo Mendes' will nor in any of the multitudinous documents regarding his property is there the slightest indication that he and João Miguez belonged to the same family. 3. Most significant of all, Immanuel Aboab (*Nomologia*, Amsterdam, 1629, p. 304) insists that he was Doña Beatrice's nephew, *su mismo sobrino*: I do not think that this term would have been applied in the sixteenth century to a nephew by marriage.

From all this, it seems certain that Joseph Nasi's father

was not one of the Mendes brothers. If, therefore, he was
Beatrice's nephew, he must have been the son of a brother
or sister of hers. The fact that they went later on by the
same name, Nasi (presumably her maiden name: for her
to have reverted to this would have been quite usual in
the circumstances), supports the former hypothesis. Indeed, the Turkish Jewish poet Saadiah Lungo, in his
elegies on members of the family, makes it clear that
Doña Beatrice and her sister, together with their two
nephews, were "relics of the house of Nasi." This would
explain, too, the contemporary statements, otherwise
incomprehensible, that it was owing to his connection
with the lady in question that Don Joseph was raised up
from poverty to affluence; he was not therefore a natural
heir to the Mendes fortunes.

As a result of the assumption that Nasi was the son of
one of the Mendes brothers, it has been deduced, and
hitherto invariably stated, that the original or "Jewish"
name of the latter also was Nasi. In view of what has been
said above, this is obviously incorrect. On the other
hand, the Duchess of Naxos, Francisco Mendes' daughter,
is referred to in a contemporary source as being a child of
Francisco Mendes Bemvisto (cf. d'Azevedo, *Historia dos
christãos novos portugueses*, p. 368; see below, page 197)
and in a Hebrew dedication as being "of the house of
Benveniste" (*Hebräische Bibliographie*, i., 67); while
Agostino Enriques, a kinsman of the family (who subsequently called himself Abraham Benveniste: see below,
page 180) speaks of her cousin as Gracia ibn Veniste
(Responsa of Joshua Soncino, § xx). Finally a Ferrara
safe-conduct, which apparently refers to them (Balletti,
Gli ebrei e gli estensi, pp. 77–8: see below, page 63), is

made out in the same name. Apparently, then, this was the authentic (and later, secret) Jewish name of the banker brothers. The latter, moreover, can it seems be more exactly identified, with the aid of the last-mentioned document, as Semah and Meir Benveniste respectively. It is upon this assumption that the present account is based. The name Mendes-Nasi, which figures confidently in such standard works as the *Jewish Encyclopaedia*, is without doubt figment of the imagination.*

Benveniste was thus the authentic Mendes *alias*, by which the family was known in Jewish circles: Nasi on the other hand was the maiden name of Doña Beatrice (to which she reverted on adopting Judaism), the married name of her daughter and the patronymic of her nephew, the Duke of Naxos.

In contrast to Diogo Mendes, the personality of his elder brother, Francisco, Beatrice's husband, barely emerges in the records. There is a faint clue to it, however, in the responsum of R. Samuel de Medina on the problem of the division of the family fortune, referred to below, p. 111. In this, he is referred to as *Rabbi Anuss* — i. e., "A Marrano Rabbi," or "A Rabbi converted by force." If the word "rabbi" is to be interpreted here literally, and not as a conventional title, we must conclude

* Lucien Wolf (*Essays in Jewish History*, page 76) speaks of Doña Beatrice's "sister-in-law, who was the widow of a former physician of the King of Portugal and . . . this widow's young son, John Micas (Miguez) . . . . afterwards Joseph Nasi" as having come to England in 1536. But the relationship he suggests is impossible, as Joseph Nasi's brother married the daughter of the lady in question, who was certainly not his sister.

that Francisco had attained — probably before the forced conversion of 1497 — a really considerable degree of Jewish scholarship and that he combined worldly and intellectual eminence in the traditional Jewish fashion, perhaps being one of the religious leaders of the Marrano community of Lisbon in this period. This overlooked epithet may therefore explain the whole course of his widow's later life.

EMPEROR CHARLES V IN 1548

AMATUS LUSITANUS

Ein Arzt von Castelblanco einer Stadt in Portugall gebürtig, hieß eigentlich Johannes
Rodriguez de Castelblanco, lebte in der Mitte des 16 Jahrhunderts, und bekante sich
zu Thessalonich zur Jüdischen Religion.

CHAPTER II

Antwerp

IT WAS in 1503 — six years after Vasco da Gama
rounded the Cape of Good Hope — that the Portuguese
sent their first spice-fleet to Antwerp. This proved a
turning-point in the city's history. The term "spice" then
covered all manner of oriental luxury products — pepper,
cinnamon, mace, nutmegs, cloves, pimento and ginger
(used medicinally), together with sandalwood (employed
as an astringent and blood-purifier), spikenard, the
oriental gum-resin known as galbanum (much appreciated
by women), wormwood, ambergris, camphor, ivory and
various other rare commodities, all valuable and some
hitherto unknown in Europe. The first cargo was sold
at so tremendous a profit that the famine feared in Portugal was averted. Others followed it at regular intervals.
Antwerp now became the center of the spice-trade in
northern Europe, this and the English cloth-trade being
the mainstay of its prosperity. A small quantity of these
"spices" continued to be imported overland by the
Venetian merchants, though not pepper, the monopoly
of which remained in the hands of the king of Portugal.
On one occasion, in 1525, a Spanish and Portuguese fleet
of quite fifty sail arrived in Antwerp in a single convoy;
and there was a period when vessels reached the harbor
almost daily from Lisbon, whence, if the winds were

favorable, it was only a ten days' voyage. The increased
supply might have been expected to bring down prices;
but owing to the vastly increased demand which now
developed and the unbridled speculation on the part of
the merchants, the price of some of these commodities
actually rose, that of pepper in particular being maintained
at a very high level, greatly to the advantage of the
Portuguese sovereign.

For all spices were not, as might be thought, merely
an accessory of luxury. In a world which knew so little
of the art of conserving foodstuffs, except with the aid of
immoderate quantities of salt, some were a necessity: a
protection to the nostrils against the all-pervading stench,
rendering palatable, though not hygienic, meat which
would otherwise have been too offensive to eat. There
was thus an unlimited market for them. The consternation at Venice at the loss of the former enormously lucrative monopoly was natural, and in 1503 the government
attempted to conclude an agreement with the Portuguese
sovereign in the hope of regulating the Calicut spice-
trade. The intermediary, who was formally thanked by
a resolution of the Council of Ten, was as it happens the
noble, much-travailed Jewish scholar-statesman, who had
once been in the Portuguese royal service and was now
an exile in Italy, Don Isaac Abrabanel. But no arrangement could divert what had by now become the normal
and natural trade-route between northern Europe and
the Far East, and the Flemish trade continued to flourish immoderately.[1]

The new arrangements proved to be of considerable
importance in European social history. Condiments
which had previously been regarded as the prerogative of

a few noblemen's houses now became a commonplace on the dining table of every well-to-do burgher. The profits of the spice-trade in the Low Countries, a royal monopoly, before long provided one quarter of the entire Indies revenue of the Portuguese Crown, which was one of the principal items in the exchequer. The fate of the lovely old city of Bruges, long the center of Flemish trade, was now sealed; Antwerp rapidly usurped its prosperity and its importance. As much business was done there in a fortnight, enviously reported the Venetian envoy about this time (though with patent exaggeration), as in his own city in an entire year.

The Portuguese colony constantly increased in consequence of all this. In 1511, the city magistrates gave that "nation" a splendid mansion on the Kipdorp to serve as the center of their activities. For the House of Mendes to neglect this rich source of profit was impossible; and in the following year Francisco Mendes sent his younger brother Diogo there (as we have seen) to open a branch establishment.[2]

As not infrequently happens in such cases, it was not long before the branch overshadowed the parent house, for the rate of profit was so great that the increment at its disposal greatly exceeded the initial capital. Working in close association with the old-established mercantile firm of Affaitati, from Cremona in Italy, the House very soon began to play a prominent role in the economic life of northern Europe. From as early as 1525, the preponderant share in the pepper and spice trade had passed under their control. Before long, they headed the great sales-syndicate which worked in conjunction with the king of Portugal, the sole importer in bulk, taking con-

signments off his hands to the value of (it was said) six,
eight and even twelve hundred thousand ducats yearly,
and disposing of them at whatever price they cared to
fix to the foreign merchants who were clamoring for the
precious commodities. In the end, as the result of buying
entire cargoes, as they did, for ready cash, they made the
king of Portugal financially dependent on them to a
great extent.

In due course, Diogo Mendes, whose special qualifica-
tions for international operations of this sort were obvious,
and who gave proof of exceptional ability, overshadowed
his Italian partners. Money, as usual, bred money. His
operations extended into Italy, France, Germany and
even England, where also he had his agents in London
and elsewhere. The small traders may have resented his
highhandedness, imagining that he was personally responsible for the high prices they had to pay; but among
the wholesalers his influence was unrivalled. In the
pepper-trade at least, in which there was hardly any
outside competition, he exercised a virtual monopoly,
however much jealous rivals might grumble. No man
enjoyed a greater influence than he did on the Bourse.
In effect he was now the Spice King of Europe.

It was impossible for him to allow his accumulated
profits to remain in his hands, and they were so vast that
not more than a fraction of them could be employed in
the firm's normal mercantile business. Antwerp, however,
was rapidly becoming at this time the financial as well as
the commercial center of northern Europe, and Diogo
Mendes proved to be a financial genius with few equals
in his day. He collaborated in business affairs with the
Fugger of Augsburg, the greatest of all banking-houses

before the age of the Industrial Revolution;[3] and, when
the king of Portugal promised the emperor money for the
Turkish War, he was able to place 200,000 florins at
the disposal of the Portuguese factor to be transmitted
to the latter by means of that famous House. He participated, too, in the loan-transactions of the English
treasury which, under Henry VIII, had become centered
in Antwerp instead of as previously in Florence, now
struggling for her existence. The capital at his disposal
was estimated at 300,000 or 400,000 florins, apart from
50,000 which he held on account of his associates at Lisbon
and what was deposited with him by his compatriots in
Flanders.[4]

A great many of the latter were, like the Mendes
family, New Christians. This was natural. The most
vital elements in the commercial world at Lisbon —
especially those interested in any new branch of enterprise — belonged to this category, and it was inevitable
that they should figure in at least a similar ratio in the
Portuguese settlements abroad. Some, moreover, finding
that they suffered at home because of their Jewish origin,
whatever their actual opinions in matters of faith, thought
it advisable to establish themselves where their antecedents were unknown; others used Antwerp as a halfway
house on their way to the lands of liberty in the Levant
for which they could not embark directly owing to ecclesiastical vigilance. As a result of the marriage between
Philip, heir to both Charles the Bold of Burgundy and the
Emperor Maximilian, with Juana the Mad, heiress to
Ferdinand and Isabella of Spain, the Low Countries were
now under the same rule as the bulk of the Iberian Peninsula (as well as south Italy and the Habsburg dominions

in Central Europe), both owing allegiance to the Holy
Roman Emperor, Charles V. The political association
between the two widely-separated geographical areas
naturally encouraged migration between them. As the
threat of the Inquisition in Portugal loomed closer, so the
influx to Antwerp grew, so that in 1525 it was found
desirable to issue instructions for all newly-arrived Portuguese to register at the Town Hall. Fearful, however, of
frightening them away entirely, in the following year the
emperor promised all who settled there temporarily that
they would not be molested on the score of religion. The
colony thus received a further impetus. The Portuguese
"New Christians" were recognized as being a highly useful element in local life. The city authorities testified, a
little later on, to their probity and utility. Their commercial morality, they said, was unexceptionable — there
were fewer bankruptcies among them than among any
other section of the population. They were conspicuously
loyal, assisting in the defense of the city in time of danger.
The commodities they imported were irreplaceable and
their commercial activities brought down the rate of
interest on the Bourse, greatly to the advantage of the
public and of the emperor himself. A contemporary
informs us how they traded in many kinds of merchandise — better, more precious and more necessary than
were commonly found — such as spices, sugars, wine,
oil, cotton, Brazil wood and ivory, and various rare
fruits, such as figs and raisins, in addition to precious
stones, jewelry, pearls, rings, gems and so on. They had
among them, too, a sprinkling of scholars and professional
men, some of whom were subsequently to make a considerable name for themselves.

Antwerp was among the most colorful and exciting cities in northern Europe at the time; and the Spanish and Portuguese colony of which the Mendes family formed part was a little world in itself. The Portuguese consul for some years was the geographer-humanist Damião de Goes, one of the most eminent of Portuguese scholars and stylists. The New Christian group included Luis Perez of Saragossa, whose son Marco was later to be at the head of the Calvinist Consistory and one of the most notable figures in the history of the Reformation in the Spanish Netherlands. Another outstanding personality was Martin Lopéz de Villanueva (uncle of the prince of French essayists, Michel de Montaigne) whose family was to show similar tendencies. The Jewish loyalties of these two were probably never very great, but the reverse was the case with young João Rodrigues of Castel-Branco,[5] who was later to acquire fame under the Latinized name of Amatus Lusitanus as one of the most distinguished physicians and medical writers of his age and ended his days, as we shall see, as a professing Jew. (His name will recur very frequently in the following pages.) He became the medical attendant to the Mendes family and records how on one occasion he treated Diogo, "the wealthiest merchant of the age," with the conserve of roses sent to him from Ferrara by Sebastian Pinto (presumably a fellow Marrano), who considered this the most fitting gift he could distribute among his princely and other especially eminent acquaintances.[6] Another distinguished New Christian physician who practiced in Antwerp at this time was Diogo Pires, of Evora (subsequently to attain a considerable reputation in the literary world for his Latin poetry, published under the inelegant name of Pyrrhus Lusitanus), who came to Flanders with Amatus and remained closely associated with him throughout his life. (He too ultimately returned to Judaism, as Isaiah Cohen.)[7] Albrecht Dürer, certainly the greatest German artist of that or perhaps any age, was on terms of considerable intimacy with the members of the New Christian circle and their friends at the time of his lengthy visit to the city in 1520–1, dining on Shrove Tuesday at the great banquet given by Martin Lopéz and receiving a present of sugar cane — then an exceptional luxury — from Ruy Fernandes, the Portuguese factor; and one may picture him, too, coming in and out of Diogo Mendes' mansion, hoping perhaps for a lucrative commission.

This, then, was the environment into which Beatrice Mendes came in 1536 after her husband's death, an attractive young widow of about twenty-six. The funds that she brought no doubt formed a useful addition to the firm's capital, and her own business acumen was very considerable. She thus began to be very closely associated with her brother-in-law in all of his activities, both commercial and personal, and there seems to have been complete sympathy between them in all things. She had brought with her a sister, Brianda,[8] apparently a little her junior; the latter now became Diogo's wife. Thus a new chapter started in the history of the Mendes family.[9]

Though so warmly Jewish in sympathy, they did not dare to show it in public, even in Antwerp. Their religious life was much the same as that of other Marranos throughout the Spanish and Portuguese dominions. They rested as far as possible on the Sabbath; they abstained from forbidden food; they ate unleavened bread on the Passover; they fasted on the Day of Atonement in accordance with the rigors of biblical law (as well as on other minor fasts, some self-imposed); they assembled for prayer from time to time in one another's households. (It is not difficult to imagine that in Antwerp the Mendes mansion was a usual meeting place.) But little more than this was possible. In order to avert suspicion, they had to attend Mass regularly, to be shriven on occasion, and to perform in public all the incidental ritual of the Roman Catholic religion. In Flanders they were perhaps able to live somewhat more freely than in the Peninsula. It was pretty generally suspected, indeed, that the New Christians were somewhat lax in their religious observances — so much so that people even spoke of a "Jews' Street" and a public synagogue in the city. But, nevertheless, the utmost circumspection was necessary, and a single false step might imperil the security of the entire family, or even the entire group.

If their Jewish enthusiasms were sincere, why did they not follow the example of so many other Marranos and go on from Antwerp to some place where they could profess their religion openly? For persons so well-known, it might not indeed have been so easy, even had they been willing to risk the loss of all their property. But apart from all this, there was another reason. By virtue of his position and wealth, Diogo was able to perform exceptionally great services to his coreligionists, in Flanders and elsewhere, which would have been impossible had he lived in any other place; and even rabbis of indubitable piety and profound scholarship were willing to concede that in these circumstances he committed no sin in re-

maining where he was, even at the price of concealing
his faith.[10]

For arrival in Antwerp was only the first stage in the
Marrano odyssey, when they escaped from the Peninsula. It remained to complete the arduous journey
southwards, over the Alps and into Italy or the Balkans
and, if possible, to convey their property as well. In the
end the House of Mendes maintained an elaborate organization all over Europe for helping the process. One of their
London agents, Christopher Fernandes, was commissioned
to board the Portuguese spice-ships when they put in at
Plymouth or Southampton and warn any Marranos who
might be aboard whether they might proceed in security
and confidence to the Low Countries, or whether danger
awaited them there for some reason. Another of the
firm's London representatives, Antonio de la Ronha, "a
tall Jew with one eye, and master of Jewish theology,"
who was related to the Mendes family, helped the fugitives to realize the property they had brought with them,
if it were necessary, and provided them with bills of exchange on Antwerp for the amount raised, so as to minimize the possibilities of confiscation and loss.[11]

In Antwerp itself, the Marrano colony centered round
the family business, in which many presumably found
employment. Moreover, every now and again parties
would be despatched southwards, from one trusty representative to another, towards the haven of refuge on
which they had decided, in Italy or Turkey. At every
stage, they could find persons to assist and counsel them.
Before they set out, they received minute instructions
as to the journey — which roads should be taken and
which avoided, what inns were safest and where help and

advice could be obtained in case of need. The transmission of property provided another problem, but the great banking-house, with its network of agencies, naturally had special facilities for solving it. Nor was collaboration confined to Jews. In Venice, for example, the underground agency was managed by the former Antwerp burgher, Daniel Bomberg, who in addition to his great work as a printer of Hebrew books (there is no Christian to whom Jewish scholarship is under a greater debt) received the property transmitted by the Mendes bank for Marranos settled in Italy, and reconsigned it to the owners.[12] The brains behind the whole of this elaborate organization, thrilling as any detective story, were Diogo Mendes and his amazing sister-in-law, Beatrice. There is nothing similar in Jewish history, or perhaps in any history, until our own day and the organization of the "underground railway" for saving Jews from the hell of Nazi and post-Nazi Europe and securing their entry (as happened in very many instances then as well) to the Land of Israel.

Direct action on behalf of the Marranos was sometimes possible too. The two kinsfolk and partners of the House of Mendes were, of course, closely associated with the attempts made by the New Christian group in Portugal to postpone or prevent the establishment of the Inquisition there, and subscribed lavishly to the interminable subscriptions that had to be raised in the hope of securing this object by way of gift or bribe. The climax came in 1535. An agreement was now reached in Portugal with the papal nuncio, Marco della Rovere, Bishop of Senigallia, for the payment to the Pope of the sum of 30,000 ducats if he would prohibit the Inquisition

entirely. But an unfortunate dispute followed. The New
Christians, smarting from previous experience, suspected
the authorities in Rome of intending to evade their side
of the bargain, and as a precaution only part of the
agreed amount was forthcoming in cash. This imperilled
the whole arrangement. In a final attempt to settle the
dispute, the nuncio returned home by way of Antwerp,
where he did his utmost to persuade Diogo and his newly-
arrived sister-in-law (who had subscribed heavily on
other occasions) to make up the deficit. But notwithstanding their open-handedness, no conclusion could be
reached; and this unfortunate dispute brought the introduction of the Holy Office into Portugal, with its calami-
tous results, appreciably nearer.[13]

As for Diogo, he had already been made to realize by
sharp experience the perpetual danger in which New
Christians stood everywhere in Christian Europe. His
great position in the commercial world at Antwerp
aroused jealousy and invited attack; and his Jewish
origin, together with his strongly-suspected Jewish sym-
pathies, placed a weapon in the hands of his enemies of
which they were not slow to avail themselves. The constant stories which reached the emperor, highly colored
and grossly exaggerated, about the number and religious
backslidings of the New Christians in Antwerp, strengthened the latter's determination to vitalize the Inquisitional procedure in his dominions. One of the first actions
of the new commissary appointed for the Low Countries
in 1530 was, therefore, to arrest Mendes and three others
on suspicion of heresy (February, 1531). They promptly
appealed to the letters of safe-conduct granted by the emperor five years before and were released on the same day.

This proved to be the preliminary skirmish in a protracted campaign, which ultimately resulted (though not
until some years had elapsed) in the complete uprooting
of the Marrano colony. The next engagement was in the
spring of the following year. It was one of the episodes,
so common in Marrano history at the time, in which
envy and fanaticism, spite and fear, all played their part.
Years before, there had arrived in the city a Portuguese
New Christian woman who was trying to get away from
her husband, one of the royal physicians at Lisbon (in
whose number so many Marranos figured even at this
early date). She entered into relations with Mendes and
his associates, who smuggled her out of the country to
Salonica, where she and her four children joined the Jewish community. Now, in May, 1532, one of the latter
came back to the Low Countries in search of his father,
after long wanderings, and told his piteous story. One
of the Mendes' commercial rivals encouraged him to
go to Bruges and repeat the details to the emperor's
confessor, who (as he rightly imagined) was profoundly —
or rather, fanatically — interested. Before long, Charles
himself was primed with the fullest possible details about
the Antwerp banker's activities and alleged misdemeanors — how he had in his hands the trust for the Portuguese
spices, how he indulged in forbidden commercial activities,
how he assisted renegades, how he was in touch with the
Jews of Turkey, how he was himself a secret Judaizer.
The emperor listened, scandalized, and ordered action to
be taken at once, his protection being now withdrawn.
In July, 1532, orders were given for the arrest of Mendes
and some of his associates on a charge of *lèse majesté*,
against God and the emperor, and a commission was

despatched by the Council of Brabant to conduct the
proceedings. As on the previous occasion, the Antwerp
authorities, aghast at this onslaught on so prominent a
figure in civic life (which created a dangerous precedent
for them all), put up obstacles. Nevertheless, though
Diogo's close friend, Gabriel de Negro, was able to escape
from the country, he himself was first placed under
house-arrest and then removed in custody to Brussels,
bail being refused.

A universal outcry followed. The city magistrates
asserted that this was a breach of the privileges contained
in their late Charter of Privileges, "the Joyous Entry,"
and claimed that they and no other were the proper
judges to try the case. The consuls of Spain, Genoa,
Florence and Lucca added their protests. The Portuguese
factor pointed out that, with Mendes in gaol, his king
could not possibly pay the Fuggers on the emperor's
account the 200,000 ducats due to them on the occasion
of the next three annual fairs, and widespread ruin and
bankruptcy would inevitably result. Damião de Goes
himself was sent with another delegate to explain the
situation to the regent, Mary of Hungary. Even Henry
VIII of England, with whom Diogo had important
treasury relations, was persuaded to intervene, and to
testify (on what basis it is not easy to see) to his orthodoxy.[14] The king of Portugal for his part, who had not
yet been paid for the last consignment of spices, instructed
his local representative to try to save something out of
the ruin, while there was still time, and to look about for
a safer trading-depot. In consequence of his representations, it was agreed to settle the prisoner's outstanding
commitments out of the sequestered property, and to

discharge all letters-of-credit standing in his name, except those to other New Christians.

As a result of the general uproar and the confusion that had ensued, it was ultimately found wisest to drop the charges of business misdemeanors. At the same time, whether for reasons of policy or through lack of definite evidence, the accusation of heresy was not pressed, Diogo maintaining indeed (as he could hardly fail to do) that although of Jewish extraction he had lived as a good Christian during the whole period of his residence in Antwerp. There remained the charge of helping fugitive Marranos; but he had a ready reply to this — it was merely a question of normal commercial operations, some of which had as a matter of fact turned out to be highly unfortunate so far as he was concerned. In view of the king of Portugal's representations, it was certainly not worth while to take drastic action on this subordinate charge. In September, 1532, accordingly, after a couple of months' imprisonment, the prisoner was released under caution-money of 50,000 ducats, his sureties being the great merchant Erasmus Schetz and three other prominent Antwerp burghers. In the end, on the payment of a substantial sum in ready cash, all proceedings were abandoned. The final outcome was not, as a matter of fact, entirely to Diogo's disadvantage, for as a result of the episode the emperor had been compelled to recognize in fact the existence of the spice monopoly, from which the accused magnate drew such rich profits.

It was four years after Diogo's arrest that Doña Beatrice arrived in Antwerp. In consequence of the recent disclosures, conditions here were now somewhat less favorable than they had once been, and alarms and excursions were renewed from time to time. In August, 1532, while her brother-in-law was awaiting trial, the emperor had issued a "Placard" forbidding admittance to the Low Countries to New Christians on their way to Turkey. As a matter of fact, thanks to the elaborate organization set up by the House of Mendes, this restriction had hardly any result; and in due course a fresh edict (issued in 1537) not only permitted persons of this class to settle in Antwerp with full rights, but even guaranteed them immunity from prosecution for offences committed elsewhere. When two years later the Holy Office opened its activities in Lisbon, a panic-stricken flight from the Peninsula began, on a far larger scale than ever before. To emigrate was indeed difficult, but it could be managed with some little exercise of resource and ingenuity. (For example, so as to avoid suspicion, entire shiploads sometimes came to the Low Countries by an absurdly devious route, via Madeira!) In Italy, the number of those who constantly arrived from Portugal now increased to such an extent that in 1540 a commission was set up at Milan, then under Spanish rule, to make a thorough investigation into the matter. The disclosures which resulted proved to be little less than sensational. In consequence, in those parts of the country which were under Spanish control or influence, wholesale arrests were now made of New Christians on their way to Ancona or Salonica, many of whom were suspected of having been furnished with funds for the journey by Diogo Mendes himself.

When this news reached Antwerp, the latter hurriedly summoned a meeting in his house to consider what steps should be taken to meet the emergency; among those present were three of the leading merchants of the city —

Manuel Lopes, Manuel Serano and Lope de Provincia —
and Antonio de la Ronha, Diogo's London agent who
had been specially summoned over to attend. It was
determined to instruct the representative of the firm at
Milan, Gonçales Gomes, to do what he could on behalf
of the prisoners and to provide for their wants in prison;
meanwhile, everything possible would be attempted in
the hope of persuading the imperial commissioners to
suspend their activities. To defray the expenses which
would obviously be involved, a relief fund was started
among those present, Antonio de la Ronha's contribution
being made partly in English crown-pieces. A draft to
the amount of 2,000 ducats on Mendes' agents was immediately prepared, and sent to Milan without delay by
special courier.[15]

Among those present at this meeting was another
employee of the firm, Gaspar Lopes, a kinsman of Diogo's,
who had also represented him formerly in London.
Shortly afterwards he was sent on business to Italy. Here
he was arrested by the Milan commissioners on a suspicion of Judaizing and, in order to save his skin, turned
informer. The secret of the recent conference in Antwerp,
of the composition of the Marrano colony there, and
even of that in England, all came out in the course of his
depositions, with the embellishment that the real object
of the relief fund was to procure the murder of the commissioners.

The repercussions throughout the Spanish dominions
were very serious. In December, the emperor, exasperated
by the disclosures, gave instructions to the margrave at
Antwerp to take drastic action against all New Christians
in the city whose orthodoxy was suspect, and summoned

the faithful to lend their assistance. The city magistrates — always nervous at the prospect of losing the
spice-trade, which was so largely in Marrano hands —
submitted a petition defending them and demonstrating
their value to the city. If there were, indeed, anything
in the allegation made against them on the score of religion, they said, surely it was wiser to keep them among
Christians, where their conduct could be watched, rather
than to risk driving them among the infidel. Nevertheless,
a convoy newly arrived from Portugal (including Diogo's
old nurse who had come over to join him) was arrested
shortly afterwards in Zealand. Ultimately, they were
released, as no definite ground could be found for proceedings against them except that they were abysmally,
and in some cases grotesquely, ignorant of their nominal
faith. The Venetian ambassador was of the opinion that
the arrests had been ordered not out of religious zeal, but
greed, for he calculated that it would be possible to mulct
the victims of 200,000 ducats. But this was out of the
question, since the wealthier members of the party had
remained in England, having been warned by Diogo's
agents of the danger that lay ahead. Meanwhile, Gabriel
Negro, who had already been accused together with
Mendes in 1532, thought it best to flee from the country —
for good, this time — leaving behind all his property,
including a fine humanistic library. The information
elicited in the course of the inquiry was communicated to
the English government, which ordered the arrest of those
persons suspected of being Jews and the sequestration
of their property. Though they were subsequently re-
stored to liberty, it was a grim warning; and before long
the little London community was broken up.[16]

There is no evidence that the Mendes were themselves
disturbed again at this time;[17] and, although Diogo apparently went into hiding for a while, we know how he was
still continuing to act, on behalf of his fellow New Christians in Portugal, as the financial intermediary for the
transmission of funds to their agent in Rome, Diogo
Fernandes Netto, in the hope of securing some modifica-
tion in the procedure of the Inquisition. (It may be that
the reason for this immunity was the recent commercial
crisis caused by the speculations in gold of one of the
Italian merchant-colony, which had shaken the credit of
the Portuguese factor and nearly involved the whole
corporation in ruin.) Nevertheless, this experience seems
to have determined Mendes and his closer associates that
life under Spanish rule was impossible for persons of their
antecedents, compelled to stifle every expression of Jewish
sentiment, and risking their lives if they did not. Doña
Gracia, above all, was bent on leaving that atmosphere
of oppression and establishing herself in some land where
she would be able to worship the God of her fathers as she
desired. She pressed her brother-in-law to come to a
decision. In the end, it was agreed between them that
they should begin to settle up their affairs forthwith
and should leave Flanders for good within twelve months
at the most, with the object of settling either in one of
the great trading-cities of Germany or in some other land
where a more tolerant atmosphere prevailed, and there
throw off the veil of Christianity and live as Jews.

But fate was against them. Before he could carry out
the agreement, Diogo died (at the end of 1542 or beginning of 1543, when his heirs are mentioned in a formal
document).[18] His will, in its public version at least, was

a model of orthodoxy as well as of benevolence. He left
the sum of 1,600 Flemish pounds for the poor, out of the
income of which one hundred pounds were to be distributed in charity each year for all time in Portugal or
(if it proved impossible to arrange this) in Flanders —
one third for the relief of needy prisoners, one third for
clothing the naked, one third for dowering orphans.[19]
(It is perhaps significant that these were considered
among the Jews to be the three primary social obligations after the promotion of study.)

In connection with the family business the testator
affirmed that one half of the capital belonged to his sister-
in-law, Doña Beatrice, according to the terms of his
brother's will and of the understanding between them.
Implicitly relying on her ability and her probity, he also
nominated her as administrator of the rest of the firm's
capital on behalf of his widow (who was to receive back
from it only her dowry-money) and his infant daughter,
not long out of her cradle. (To the former he gave no
voice whatsoever in the management of his estate, having
already experienced perhaps the volatility of tempera-
ment of which she was to give such ample proof later on.)
Thus Beatrice Mendes was made the administrator of
one of the greatest fortunes and one of the greatest
businesses in Europe. Her dream of leaving Flanders
could not in consequence be realized as yet: there was
too much to be settled, too much to be arranged, too
many interests to consider. More and more she leaned
for advice and help henceforth on the elder of her two
nephews, João Miguez. He now began to travel about
Europe in connection with the affairs of the firm and
became a familiar figure in the principal trading cities —

especially Lyons, than as now one of the centers of the
silk industry, and in consequence of this, of international
banking and finance. Another of the inexperienced young
widow's mainstays was a kinsman of her husband's belonging to the family of Benveniste, Agostino Enriques
(his name will often recur later, in the end in a somewhat
sinister connection), who was also in the employ of the
firm. It was on the advice of these two that her brother-
in-law in his will instructed her to rely, and they were to
have the administration of his estate should she be compelled to relinquish it for any reason.

Thus the business continued to flourish, the firm of the
"Heirs of Francis and Diogo Mendes" remaining a power
in the financial world and continuing to take its share in
government loans, English and continental.[20]

Fresh proceedings against Diogo for heresy had perhaps
been in contemplation at the time of his death, being
delayed only in order to collect overwhelming evidence.
From the point of view of the imperial treasury, they
would obviously have been lucrative, for a condemnation
on this charge entailed automatically the confiscation of
a man's entire property. (It was this that gave the
Inquisition much of its impetus, as well as much of its
horror.) It did not seem equitable that his death should
involve the emperor in loss; and posthumous proceedings
were therefore opened against him. Doña Beatrice
fought courageously against the danger, piling up evidence of his unimpeachable orthodoxy, bringing witnesses
to prove his Christian zeal, placating the officials with
gifts of money, using every possible expedient and spar-
ing no reasonable expense; there was obviously no other
course that could be taken, save to accept defeat and

confiscation. In the end, it was agreed to withdraw the
charge, with its somewhat problematical outcome, on
condition that she lent the emperor the sum of 100,000
ducats free of interest for two years to meet his most
pressing requirements.[21] (The tragedy of Charles V's
long reign was that he was constantly in desperate financial straits, hardly able to raise the money to carry on the
essential work of government.) It was a great, but, in
view of her wealth, by no means a crushing sum that was
involved. She had opposed governmental greed, wearing
the mask of religious zeal, by adroitness, casuistry and
lavish use of money; and she had been victorious. This
was the first of her long series of triumphs. But it proved
a dangerous precedent.

In the resplendent but by no means exclusive court of
the queen regent in Brussels, the enormously wealthy
widow, still young and still attractive, found a cordial
welcome. Her elder nephew, João Miguez, was admitted
to the circle of the regent's nephew, Maximilian (later
Holy Roman Emperor), becoming his occasional companion and tilting partner and acquiring a taste for
courtly accomplishments which was to stand him in good
stead throughout his life. Her daughter, Brianda or
Reyna, was universally courted for her exceptional
beauty, as well as for the great fortune which would one
day be hers. Even her niece, Diogo's young daughter,
who was hardly more than a baby, began to be considered
in the marriage market, in accordance with the spirit of
an age when contracts of matrimonial alliance were sometimes concluded, in more august circles, between children
not yet conceived. The queen regent had her own ideas
on the subject, regarding the young heiresses in the light

of prizes to be conferred on nobles whom she and the emperor wished to reward or favor; and there was at one time some talk of bringing them up in court and marrying them off without any regard to what they or their mothers felt about it.[22]

Though this threat was averted, the importunity of suitors remained. The most pressing and most favored among them was Don Francisco d'Aragon, son of one Nuño Manuel and an illegitimate descendant of the Aragonese royal house. Many years before he had accompanied the Empress Isabella on her first coming to Spain from Portugal, and though he was long past the prime of youth, this service commended him particularly to the emperor. As commissary general to investigate various charges against the New Christians not long since, he had the opportunity to become familiar with the circumstances of the lovely orphan, Beatrice's daughter. He now pressed his claim with the damsel, with the mother and with the emperor himself, to whom he promised no less than 200,000 ducats on loan, out of his wife's coffers, if the marriage took place. It was equivalent to a promise to share the spoil; and on April 28, 1544, Charles sent a letter to his sister, by the suitor's own hand, warmly commending the plan and suggesting that she should have for her treasury one quarter of the anticipated sum, on which he already counted with bland confidence.

The queen regent, however, knew something of Doña Beatrice's character and fixity of purpose; and her reply to this communication was by no means encouraging. She of course promised to do what she could and proposed to speak to the mother on the subject when she was next in Antwerp. But it would not be easy. They had already had one encounter, in which she herself had been worsted, and the lady in question had the knack of avoiding awkward summonses to Court, when she did not wish to come, on the score of ill-health. Don Francisco, all eager, suggested that the mother should be disregarded and the arrangements concluded without consulting her; but this seemed to Mary highly inadvisable, as the wealthy Antwerp merchants would without doubt rise as one man against the dangerous precedent of autocratically settling their most intimate family affairs and disposing of their fortunes, and might perhaps withdraw from the country. It is a delicious picture, of the all-powerful ex-Queen of Hungary, Regent of the Netherlands, sister and deputy of the Holy Roman Emperor, trembling at the prospect of an awkward conversation with the still young, but apparently very determined, Marrano business-woman.

In due course, nevertheless, she found herself in Antwerp and obediently broached the question. Doña Beatrice, fervent Jewess that she was at heart, had no intention of allowing her daughter to marry an "Old Christian" and be lost to her faith. She did not dare to say this openly, but it was possible for her to express her views about the prospect of her becoming the wife of an elderly wastrel. She did not mince words. She would rather, she said, see the damsel dead.[23]

The matter did not, of course, end with this. Don Francisco still pressed his cause. Time after time, the emperor wrote to the regent, and the regent excused herself to the emperor. The latter now agreed that it would be inadvisable to use highhanded methods. His sister at one stage had the brilliant idea of solving the problem by obtaining the sum required from Doña Beatrice herself

by way of loan, and leaving the question of her daughter's
marriage in her hands. Conversations continued intermi-
nably — the emperor temporizing, the regent hesitating,
Don Francisco importuning, Doña Beatrice procrastinat-
ing. Suddenly, one day, towards the close of 1544[24] it was
discovered that the Mendes mansion in Antwerp was
empty of its principal inhabitants. Doña Beatrice, realiz-
ing that it was impossible to hold out indefinitely against
the emperor and his representative, had left the city on
the pretext of taking the waters at Aachen (Aix-la-Chapelle); her sister and the two damsels had accompanied her,
together with such of their treasure as they could carry
in their baggage. They had now gone beyond their ostensible destination and obviously had no intention of
returning. Before long they appeared in Venice. But the
last act of the melodrama in Antwerp had not yet been
played.

It had been impossible to realize the bulk of the family
fortune at such short notice; and it was left consequently
in the custody of João Miguez, who henceforth takes a
more and more prominent share in the affairs of the
House. The precipitate departure of the female members
of the family had obviously been suspicious, but it was
not in itself more that a formal offense, if it was an offense
at all. On the other hand, it placed the 200,000 ducats,
on which the emperor had counted, almost out of reach
unless action were taken very promptly. But on what
charge? One was always to hand when persons of New
Christian families were concerned — that of Judaizing,
which had been brought up at intervals against Diogo
Mendes both before and after his death; and the circumstances of the flight made this seem highly plausible.

Accordingly, the two widows were now accused of apostasy from the Holy Catholic faith and summoned to
answer the charge before the Council of Brabant. Since
they did not appear within the stipulated time, an embargo was placed on their property, including forty treas-
ure-filled coffers they had left in Antwerp and three
more in Germany — a veritable windfall for the depleted
imperial exchequer.

A protracted tussle now began between the government and João Miguez, all of whose subtlety and powers
of persuasion had to be called into play. He pleaded that
the widows being Portuguese subjects, their prosecution
in Antwerp was illegal; while the confiscation of their
property was unjustified, for merchant strangers such as
they were had a perfect right to leave whenever they
pleased, together with all their chattels. Even if this were
not the case, it was only a technical misdemeanor at the
worst. It was preposterous, moreover, in these circumstances, to expect the defendants to make the long and
perilous journey back over the Alps to answer to the
charges brought against them; for they had never been
considered as other than good Christians, as could easily
be confirmed by enquiry at Venice. Indeed (obviously, his
tongue was in his cheek when he wrote this) he, their
kinsman, was prepared to face the most searching examination on this account, confident that there was not a
breath of suspicion against him. After all, he added, inconsequentially, the widows were not so very wealthy,
having been left only 15,000 ducats apiece; all the rest
belonged to the girls, who were too young to be prosecuted. If this ridiculous matter were pressed to an
extreme, the foreign merchant body as a whole might

take alarm and leave Antwerp. He did not want to be unreasonable, and suggested a compromise: if the embargo on the Mendes property were removed and the proceedings quashed, he would be prepared to make the Crown a loan of, not indeed 200,000 ducats, but say 20,000 or 30,000 on the usual terms. This offer, of course, appeared ridiculous to the regent, who demanded at least 100,000 ducats — an amount which according to Miguez represented two thirds of the entire Mendes fortune. 50,000, he said, might be considered, but not a penny more. Meanwhile, more and more time was being gained.

By now, Beatrice had set to work in Venice where she was at present settled. As it happened, the German merchants who had custody of some of the disputed treasure-coffers had property of their own here, and she had managed to get this sequestered by the Venetian government by way of compensation. In order to recover it, the merchants (who had enlisted the sympathy of the Cardinal of Augsburg), handed over the coffers to the local agent of the firm of Mendes, one Jerome Zoller, to be forwarded to the owners. On examination at the frontier, it was discovered that the contents, the declared value of which was only 100 florins, included pearls and other precious objects worth a very large sum. Meanwhile, Miguez had gone, in June, 1546, to have an audience at Ratisbon with the emperor who, it seems, knighted him about this time — a much-coveted honor.[25] The latter, hard-pressed for money as always, was persuaded that a substantial sum in cash was more important to him than the prospects of glittering advantages some time in the future, and accepted 30,000 crowns in settlement of all claims. The queen regent, who had been offered nearly twice as much not long since, was furious and refused to release the sequestered property until the Council had examined the agreement and decided on its authenticity.

A protracted, preposterous and undignified bargaining now began among the three parties.[26] Miguez pleaded innocence on the one hand and poverty on the other, offering relatively inconsiderable sums for a prompt settlement. The emperor craftily professed himself willing to comply, with the intention (as he shamelessly admitted to his sister) of gaining a little ready money, but subsequently starting a further prosecution for heresy. The regent, for her part, began to press for total confiscation, frankly confessing that, in default of this, she would be unable to balance her accounts or even to return in due course any of the sequestered property other than the house and furniture; as she reminded the emperor, there was already an outstanding debt of 100,000 which had been lent him by the Mendes family in 1543, and she did not know how this sum could possibly be raised otherwise. Alarmed at this new menace, Miguez now offered to advance Charles an additional 200,000 livres for a year, free of interest, in return for a final settlement (obviously, his previous estimate of the total of the family fortune had been, to say the least, an understatement). It was a highly tempting suggestion, but even this did not at this stage satisfy the emperor, increasingly unwilling to forego the spiritual solace of prosecution for heresy and the financial benefits that might accrue from it . . . . .

And so the letters passed backwards and forwards between the emperor and the regent on the one hand, the regent and the adroit Portuguese on the other, until Miguez, too, suddenly left the country, whether openly or in secret. It is not quite clear how the matter had ended, and whether a composition had been reached or no. Most probably he had managed in the interval to realize the property of the firm little by little, and to convey it out of the country in devious ways; though perhaps the end came with a precipitate flight, leaving everything behind. In any case, what was saved out of the wreckage was very considerable indeed. The Mendes sisters were no longer living under Spanish rule, in the "iron cauldron," but in the relatively free atmosphere of Italy, despite their losses still wealthy beyond the dreams of normal avarice.

CHAPTER III

Venice

BEFORE leaving Flanders towards the close of 1544, the Mendes sisters had secured through their Italian agents, in deepest secrecy, a safe-conduct to come to Venice, together with their daughters, their households and their property. The journey across Europe was made apparently with a huge train and in a leisurely fashion. Their stay in Aix-la-Chapelle, where they first went on the pretext of taking the waters, was no doubt short, as that city was under the emperor's authority and it was not unlikely that steps might have been taken for their extradition or the opening of proceedings against them there. For the same reason, presumably, it seemed wiser not to proceed by the direct route across the Alps by way of Augsburg, usually followed by merchants, notwithstanding the presence in the city of the Fuggers, long-standing business associates of the house of Mendes. Instead, they crossed over from the Low Countries into France and made what was apparently a somewhat protracted sojourn at Lyons. Here, the center of European banking at this time, there was an influential colony of Spanish and Portuguese Marranos; moreover, the firm had important business interests, which had been developed recently under the direction of João Miguez. Thence, by slow stages, the family made its way across northern Italy to their destination.

Current rumor added a spice of romance to the story. It was said that João Miguez and Beatrice's young daughter had fallen in love, and that he had seized the opportunity to elope with her to Venice, the mother following after them in pursuit. But this was untrue, though not without a substratum of verisimilitude. Aunt and nephew worked together at all times in perfect amity and collaboration, and in fact the young gallant remained behind in, or else returned to, Antwerp in order to represent her interests, as we have seen. It is not, however, altogether out of the question that this story was deliberately put about, in order to provide a colorable pretext for the family's sudden, and suspicious, translocation.

It was not in the ghetto of Venice, among the Jews, that they took up their residence. The "tribes of the wandering foot and weary breast" had been eyed askance by the Venetian patricians throughout the Middle Ages — obviously more through economic jealousy than because of the religious zeal which they professed. It was only during the past generation that they had been tolerated in the city (nominally, on a renewable ten-year term) and they were still uncertain of their status.[1] Nor were they allowed to live in the city at large, having been herded together in 1516 in the area known by the name of the Foundry, or Ghetto, which formerly existed there — the prototype of the Jewish quarter enforced by law and rigidly cut off from the outside world, which was to become universal in Italy later on. Though the community was already of some importance, its tenure was even now to some extent precarious. Moreover, in view of the fact that the Marranos had been banished from the city in 1497, it was a little venturesome for newly-arrived Spanish and Portuguese refugees to associate themselves with it. To do so would indeed have been equivalent to a public announcement of apostasy from Christianity; and this in turn would have made possible (if not probable) not only prosecution, but also the confiscation of all property held elsewhere in Christendom. Accordingly, the Mendes family took up its residence, still ostensibly as Christians, in the center of the town, near the *Zecca* (Mint); and their house became once more, as it had been in Antwerp, the center for Marrano refugees who came to or passed through the city.

Life in Venice was colorful at this time as at no other period of her history. Her architectural development was almost completed, and the dream-city of the lagoons presented (with certain reservations, indeed) much the same general picture as it does today. The most famous of the palaces on the Grand Canal were completed and thronged with never-ending files of visitors and lackeys, diversified by timid, yellow-hatted Jews from the Ghetto. Titian, Tintoretto, Veronese, all at the height of their capabilities, were filling the picture galleries of the nobility with superb portraits and the churches with dramatic frescoes. Merchants from the four corners of the world came to traffic on the Fondachi — guttural Germans, turbanned Orientals, supercilious Frenchmen, fair-skinned Englishmen and swarthy Spaniards, most of whom were suspected of being secret Jews. The *Serenissima Dominante* was well past her prime; for the sea-route to India had been discovered, and she no longer controlled, as in a former day, the world's most lucrative markets and sources of supply. Nevertheless, this was not generally realized, and she was still considered a power in world politics. The stately pageants of the Republic — the wooing of the Adriatic, the succession of saint's days, the public spectacles on the lagoon — still gave the illusion of reality; it was not yet realized that there was little behind the sparkle, the former lusty, lovely adventuress having degenerated into a mere harlot. It was a wonderful city to visit — especially for women: and situated as they were, the Mendes sisters and their daughters had the opportunity of enjoying this life to the full.

We know little, however, of the details. It seems that here they generally went by the name of De Luna. (It may be that this was in order to avoid the attention which was inevitably attracted by the name of Mendes, notoriously associated with the world-famous Antwerp business-house.) Once more they now came into contact with the physician João Rodrigues (Amatus Lusitanus), who had formerly attended on Diogo Mendes at Antwerp. Doña Beatrice, apparently something of a valetudinarian (it was in keeping with her character), fell ill during her stay here and was treated by her own physician with an overdose of the attar of roses which had once proved so beneficial to her brother-in-law; to his great satisfaction, Amatus was able to give her sounder advice.[2]

All this time she had been living with her sister, Madonna Brianda[3] (as she was called), Diogo Mendes' widow, and looking after her interests. The latter was clearly of a very different type — selfish, volatile, irresponsible. Moreover, she greatly resented the elder sister's authority, which doubtless prevented her from enjoying Venice and Venetian life to the full. Beatrice's husband, Francisco, the founder of the family fortunes, had left her and their daughter a large interest in the property of the firm. Diogo had nominated her by his will (as we have seen) administrator of his entire estate, until his daughter married or became of age, giving his own wife no voice whatsoever. Beatrice thus controlled the entire Mendes fortune. She was dominant, and she was not a woman of the type to surrender her domination; Brianda (who received only her dowry-money) was not more than a cipher. In this new environment, seduced perhaps by the exciting world of fashion around her, she began to feel and to resent her dependence. She now demanded in her daughter's name the half share of the family property to which she considered her entitled. Beatrice, with a duty towards her niece to consider as well as her own position, refused to yield. In the end, there was a bitter quarrel between the two.

When this happened in Marrano circles there was always the danger of being tempted to use the hazardous and double-edged weapon that lay constantly to hand — a denunciation on the score of secret Judaizing. This happened time after time in the history of the period, but never perhaps in circumstances quite like this. Brianda shamelessly denounced her own sister before the courts as a Judaizer, alleging that she had come to Venice only in order to settle her affairs, after which she intended to go to Turkey with all her property, and there declare herself a Jewess — a manifest loss both to the Republic and to Christian orthodoxy. Such a person was clearly unsuited to have the tutelage of a minor; and she asked that steps be taken in order to end this state of affairs and to make her, Brianda, her daughter's guardian instead of her sister.

On the surface, this did not appear preposterous, or
even excessive. But the results went far beyond anything that she could have anticipated. The cupidity of
the Venetian government was aroused. Here, temporarily under its control, was one of the greatest fortunes
of the day; it seemed deplorable that it should be transferred into the power of the enemy of the Republic and of
Christendom. While the lawsuit brought by Brianda
was pending, an embargo was therefore placed on all the
family property; and, to make assurance surer, Doña
Beatrice was placed under arrest to prevent her from
escaping. As for her daughter, as well as her niece, it was
desirable for them to be brought up in a genuinely Christian environment and under completely unimpeachable
influences. The papal legate in Venice accordingly placed
the girls in a nunnery, away from both mothers.

Meanwhile, Brianda had been continuing her intrigues
elsewhere. A great proportion of the capital of the firm
had been in France, where its banking business had been
flourishing and considerable sums had been lent to the
government. She hoped naturally to get her daughter's
share of this, too, under her control, and used the same
method as she had at Venice, her agent being a Christian
of notorious anti-Jewish tendencies. The king of France
was, of course, happy to have the opportunity to place an
embargo on the property standing in Beatrice's name,
on the pretext of her questionable orthodoxy. But once
this sort of thing was begun, there were no limits to it.
The agent, dissatisfied with his share of the loot, realized
that Doña Brianda was as susceptible to attack on the
score of religion as her sister and, on his return to France,
after an unsatisfactory interview, denounced her as well

on the same score. As a result, her claim to that portion which she considered to be hers by right was also endangered, an embargo being now placed on this in addition to all the rest.

Once more — for the third or fourth time in the course of the decade — the family was involved in legal proceedings in which the whole of its property down to the last farthing was at stake — ostensibly on the score of heresy, in fact as the result of sheer greed and the hope of confiscation. Once more, a judicial enquiry was opened, to drag out month after month. Once more, there had to be protestations of orthodoxy, a vast outlay of money, interminable pleadings, judicious gifts, expensive certificates of unimpeachable religious observance, constant backdoor intrigues. But, on this occasion, there was also, for once, powerful external support.

Doña Beatrice's object for a long time past had been to settle in Turkey, where she would be able to revert openly and without fear to the religion of her fathers; and her only reason for delay was to be able to settle her affairs. Long since, she had sent such property as she could, little by little, to her agents in Constantinople, where her arrival was already eagerly expected. Moreover, she had here some influential friends. Among them was Moses Hamon, the sultan's physician. He was a typical figure of this generation. A native of Granada, he had been brought as a baby to Turkey on the expulsion of the Jews from Spain and had been brought up by his father, Joseph Hamon, physician to the Sultan Selim I, likewise to the calling of medicine. From his youth upwards he had served in the same capacity this sultan and his successor, Suleiman the Magnificent, now on the

throne, who exempted him and his family from all taxation. He enjoyed exceptionally great influence at the
Sublime Porte, and his coreligionists knew him as a stead-
fast Jew, a supporter of every Jewish cause and a munificent patron of scholarship. It was not difficult to arouse
his interest in the case, João Miguez doubtless acting as
the intermediary and priming him with the facts of the
episode by letter. It may be true, moreover, that (as was
suggested at the time) he hoped to arrange a match
between Beatrice's daughter, the greatest Jewish heiress
of the age, and his son Joseph, Court physician after him
and later an active member of the famous circle of
Hebrew poets at Constantinople.

Whether or not this is the case, it is unlikely that the
additional encouragement was requisite. Hamon had no
difficulty in bringing the story to the notice of the sultan
and his advisers, pointing out the great advantage that
would accrue to the Ottoman empire through the immigration of these extraordinarily affluent refugees and the
transference of their wide-spread business interests to the
Golden Horn. As the result of his persuasiveness, the
sultan began to regard the Mendes family as his own
subjects *in posse*, as it were, and thus under his protection.
It was all highly irregular, no doubt, and could hardly be
sustained in international law. But the Turkish empire
was now at the height of its power, and Venice well
advanced on its catastrophic decline and unable to risk
ill-feeling or to resist diplomatic pressure on the part of
the power with which it had recently been compelled to
sign a disastrous peace.

The sultan made it quite manifest, indeed, that he
regarded the matter as one of considerable political mo-

ment. Foreign diplomatic observers, on the other hand, watched what was happening with interest not unmingled with anxiety — especially the French, who were at that time in alliance with Turkey against the emperor, and were nervous lest some misunderstanding should throw Venice, with her still powerful fleet and her important overseas empire, into the latter's arms and thus ensure him the command of the Mediterranean. In July, 1549, the ambassador at Venice, M. de Morvilliers, began one of his despatches home with the news that he had heard from his colleague in Constantinople that a Court Messenger (*chaus*)[4] from the sultan would shortly be arriving in Venice "sent there to request this government to dispatch a certain foreign person to Constantinople, or else comply with his demands — a matter they will not find agreeable."

A subsequent communication of the ambassador's went into the subject in greater detail: —

The *bailo*[5] of this government in Constantinople informs them that the principal reason for the despatch of the special envoy is to ask them in the name of the sultan to hand over to him the Portuguese, Mende(s), together with her daughter and her property, to take them with him to Constantinople. Rumor adds that the said Mendes has married her daughter, or promised her, to the son of a certain Hamon, a Jew, physician to the Grand Signior, who favors him more than any other person of his own creed. About this matter there is a great deal of talk, to the dishonor and prejudice of the said Mendes. The substance is that it is now clear that (as has indeed always been suspected) she and all her tribe has been and is one of the sect of the Marranos, having pretended to be Christian, in order to become rich by trading freely with all merchants. . . .

When, in due course, the *chaus* arrived, it became apparent that Hamon's enthusiasm (if indeed the démarche was due to him) had exceeded his judgment, or

at any rate Doña Beatrice's desires. It was not good for
persons situated as she and her family were to venture,
except as a last resort, on so ostenatious a course, which
would draw yet further attention upon them and their
affairs. They had become accustomed to work behind
the scenes — to placate a person here, to win over another there, and to obtain their objects without declaring
themselves too positively on the one side or the other.
If the sultan's object was achieved, and they were allowed
to leave Venice through his direct intervention, they
would have to go to Turkey immediately, they would have
to declare all their property, they would risk arousing his
cupidity as well; and in the end they might lose everything they possessed. They preferred to distribute their
property as widely as possible, for the moment at least,
so that whatever happened in one country (and they
were certain of none) they would have something elsewhere on which they could count. To become virtually
Turkish-protected subjects was, moreover, inadvisable
for the moment; for there was still much to be done in
Italy to settle up the affairs of the House, and meanwhile
in case of renewed war between the Cross and the Crescent they would run very serious risk. By following the
same methods which had proved successful before in
Flanders, they had already, as a matter of fact, solved the
immediate problem though at heavy cost.

For by this time, Doña Beatrice was no longer domiciled in Venice. In consequence perhaps of the preliminary representations made by the Turkish government,
perhaps of her lavish expenditure of money, she had been
released from confinement, at the beginning of 1549, and
reunited with her daughter. They had, however, been

given to understand that, unless they solemnly undertook to comport themselves as true Christians henceforth, they would no longer be allowed to live in Venice or the Venetian territory, a month only being given them to decide.

The recurrent crises of the past few years must have determined Doña Beatrice that a life of constant dissimulation was not worth while. Unprepared as yet to leave Italy, she made her way, together with her daughter, to Ferrara, under a special safe-conduct from the duke, in whose dominions (as we shall see) persons of her stock were cordially welcomed and were, moreover, assured of immunity from any prosecution on religious grounds. ("The elder [sister] who has the entire administration of all the property, retired to Ferrara seven or eight months ago,[6] under an ample safe-conduct received from the duke," reported the French envoy, on July 12th, at the close of the despatch cited above.)

But mother and daughter did not go alone, for a great surprise was in store for the contemporary diplomatic observers. At this stage, Beatrice's flighty, selfish, unsettled younger sister, Brianda, who had been responsible in the first instance for all the recent trouble, who had denounced her as a Judaizer, who had gone out of her way to declare her Christian allegiance, now had her opportunity. She could remain in Venice living in patrician circles, and enjoying fashionable life to the full: for, even if she was only able to secure control of a limited proportion of the family fortunes, she would be able to maintain herself in affluence and to secure a glittering match for her daughter. But recent events had shown her perhaps how little Christian benevolence counted in sixteenth-century Italy when greed came into play; per-

haps her momentary experience of ecclesiastical orthodoxy had disappointed her; perhaps she was encouraged
by the support from Constantinople, which demonstrated
to her that there was still high hope elsewhere; perhaps
she had begun to feel genuine twinges of conscience, or
her own daughter — subsequently to show herself a
devoted Jewess — had aroused her better feeling. It is
even conceivable that the whole thing had been from the
outset an involved plot to secure the family property to
one of the two sisters by vindicating her unquestioned
orthodoxy, with results that had gone further than was
originally anticipated. Whatever the reason, to the
general surprise, within a very short while, Brianda and
her daughter joined the elder sister in Ferrara. When
the sultan's special envoy arrived at Venice, they came
back there to meet him, this time under the double protection of the duke of Ferrara and of the Turkish emperor.

The French ambassador reported the sequel to his
royal master, as a matter of high importance: —

The [younger] sister of this Mendes has left secretly with
her daughter and gone to join the other in Ferrara. In view of
the great hatred that they formerly showed against one another this increases the suspicion against them; for it seems
that the danger of the possible embarrassment to themselves
or their property has suddenly reconciled them. Some say, that
the elder Mendes has sent to intercept the *chaus* in order to
prevent him from coming any further. It is also said that about
six weeks ago she despatched her most trusted agent to France
to realize and withdraw as much as possible of her funds at
Lyons and other places in your realm.

All these things are so obscure to me that I cannot find out
the truth. Nevertheless, it is obvious that there is some hid-
den mystery, because these women were greatly troubled when
they heard the news of the approaching arrival of the *chaus*;
and I have ascertained from an excellent source that they sent
express messengers to speak to him about it, and another as

far as Constantinople. It is thought that this was done in order
to stop the *chaus* and to make him do nothing until they obtain
other instructions from Constantinople, so that he will not
discuss their affairs with the government here without their
approval. At the present moment, since neither they nor
their property are in the government's hands, the intervention
of the Grand Signior cannot be of any advantage to them, but
may on the contrary do serious harm.

In any case, it was now pointless for them to continue
to live in Venice. The affairs of the family were in order,
and as much property as possible had now been withdrawn from Christian Europe and was in safe custody
elsewhere. The long-drawn dispute in the Netherlands
over what had been left behind, which might have ended
disastrously had it been possible to produce definite evidence that the principal personages involved were Judaizing, was now ended. Moreover — partly as the result
of the attention attracted by what had recently happened
in connection with the Mendes family, partly owing to
the persistent enmity of Emperor Charles V against the
New Christians — the Venetian Senate had issued a decree on July 8, 1550, ordering the immediate interruption
of all commercial relations between their subjects and
the Marranos, who were to leave the city within two
months; and this was implemented a month later by an
order to the *censori* of the Republic to collaborate with
the Inquisition in taking proceedings against those whose
Christian orthodoxy was suspected. There was to be a
reversal of policy barely a generation later, when Fra
Paolo Sarpi conducted his famous polemic against the
Holy Office; and Venice was to become for a time, towards
the end of the sixteenth century and the beginning of
the seventeenth, the principal European city of refuge
for these persecuted elements. Nevertheless, for the mo-

ment, its doors were closed, regardless of what suffering
was caused. Hard by, however, on the *terra ferma*, there
was an alternative asylum, whence Doña Beatrice, now
in safety, watched the tragedy with an agonized heart
and did whatever was humanly possible to succor the
sufferers.

It seems that negotiations had already been opened up
on their behalf with the duke of Ferrara a little while
previous through the medium of a certain Rabbi Yomtob
(perhaps Yomtob Atias, the printer, *alias* Jeronimo de
Vargas, who was of Portuguese birth),[7] some delay having
been granted so as to enable her to settle up her affairs
elsewhere. Now, letters-patent were issued to the family,
on February 12, 1550, welcoming her and her associates
to the city, and guaranteeing them substantial privileges.
It was solemnly promised that they were not to be
molested on the score of religion, even though they might
formerly have lived under the guise of Christians. They
were to be allowed to practice Judaism and to conduct
themselves according to the rites of Jewish tradition.
Like others, they were to be allowed to have slaves for
their service, who were not to be taken from them without payment on the pretext of being made Christians.
If the letters-patent were to be withdrawn by the duke's
successor, they were to be allowed eighteen months to
settle their affairs and to leave, taking with them all their
property, duty free.

They thus came to Ferrara, not as ostensible Christians, but as Jews. This was the first time that their
Jewish names were officially used, the document being
issued in the names of "Donna Vellida [wife] of Don
Semer Benveniste and Donna Reina [wife] of Don Meir

Benveniste," with all their families and households.[8] In the event, however, they preferred to be called, not by their husbands' name of Benveniste, but by the ancestral appellation of Nasi; and it is as Doña Gracia Nasi that our principal character was henceforth known.[9]

A new chapter now opened in her life. She was no longer a Marrano, but a proud, eager, almost chauvinistic Jewess.

CHAPTER IV

Ferrara

THE bustling city of Ferrara was at this time at the height of its prosperity and fame, under the rule of that typical Renaissance paladin, Duke Ercole II, of the House of Este. This ducal line, combining close autocratic rule with an exceptionally enlightened economic regime, tried to enhance the prosperity of their dominions by encouraging immigration as much as possible as a cardinal point of public policy. The nationality and creed of those who came were to them a matter of indifference, so long as they could contribute to the general welfare.

There was a relatively old-established colony of Italian Jews in the city, whose numbers had been augmented in the course of the fifteenth century by arrivals from Germany fleeing from the persecutions endemic in that land. In 1492, a handful of refugees from Spain, barbarously treated elsewhere, found a warm welcome in the Este dominions and set up a synagogue following the Iberian (Sephardi) rite in the capital. As early as 1538, asylum had been offered to Portuguese Marranos as well, and when, in 1540, the arrests took place in the duchy of Milan, a certain Solomon de Ripa was sent there by the duke to secure the release of those who could legitimately claim his protection.[1] By now, the colony had attained numbers and distinction. Time after time, scandalized

Catholics or disappointed renegades, returning to the
Peninsula, gave an account of men they had encountered
there frequenting the "Portuguese" synagogue and
known as Jews, though it was notorious in the city that
they had lived formerly as Catholics at Lisbon or Coimbra.

This was the environment in which the Nasi family
settled on leaving Venice in 1549/50 — the two sisters,
Gracia and Reyna (as they must now be called): their
young daughters, named with sororal reciprocity Reyna
and Gracia respectively (the latter, it is reported, was
called Gracia *la chica*, or "The Small," for the sake of
differentiation).[2] Their nephew, João Miguez, was, it
seems, only an occasional visitor, at the best; but his
younger and less vigorous brother now joined the family
circle, also reverting to Judaism under the name of Samuel
Nasi (his former appellation is unknown). He later es-
poused his young cousin Gracia, Doña Reyna's daughter,
who was henceforth also known as Gracia Nasi.[3] It was
a typical expedient to keep the family fortune in the
family; but it had the incidental result of establishing
that volatile young lady firmly in Judaism.

The outstanding personality in the community at the
time of Doña Gracia's arrival in the city was, as it happens, another woman — it is to be hoped her friend,
although her rival. This was Doña Benvenida, a member
of the great Jewish family of Abrabanel which, on the
expulsion of the Jews from Spain, had originally settled in
Naples. She was the daughter of Don Jacob, brother of
the famous Don Isaac Abrabanel, the philosopher-states-
man, who was as familiar with the courts of Europe as
with the profundities of Holy Writ. Her husband was
Don Samuel, Isaac's son, long the head of Neapolitan

THE SEPHARDI SYNAGOGUE AT FERRARA
founded 1493; destroyed 1944

DUKE ERCOLE II OF FERRARA

Jewry, of whom contemporaries said that he was *Trismegistos* or Thrice Great — great in knowledge of the Torah, great in nobility and great in wealth — and that he combined all the characteristics which, according to tradition, are requisite for the gift of prophecy. His wife shared his great qualities. Don Pedro de Toledo, the viceroy of the kingdom of Naples for the Spanish sovereign, thought so highly of her that she was associated in the education of his second daughter, Leonora, who (it is told) called her "mother," and continued to turn to her for advice even after she became grand duchess of Tuscany. This association may have postponed but could not avert the expulsion of the Jews from Apulia and southern Italy, at the insistence of the implacable Emperor Charles V, in 1541; and the family then settled in Ferrara, being eagerly welcomed there by the reigning duke.

Here the Abrabanels lived in magnificent style. Their affairs continued to flourish. Their charity was on a princely level. Their mansion was a center of cultural life, thronged by Jewish savants and well frequented by Christians also. When Don Samuel died in 1547 through taking an overdose of scammony (Amatus Lusitanus tells the story)[4] his widow continued his business on a grand scale, securing important commercial privileges in Tuscany thanks to her relations with that Court. Her Jewish sentiment was as profound and eager as might have been anticipated from a member of that great house. When a remarkable apocalyptic pretender, David Reubeni, had come to Italy on a pretended mission on behalf of the lost tribe of Reuben (of which his brother, he said, was king), she had been his most eager supporter,

and he carried with him on his travels a magnificent
silken banner, embroidered in gold with the Ten Commandments, which she had worked for him with her own
hands. The report of her profound religious feeling and
her many acts of charity penetrated as far as Egypt and
the Holy Land. She was deeply pious, and indulged in
frequent fasting. It was her delight to dower penniless
orphans. No poor person who came to her house was
ever turned away. She was a munificent patroness of
learning. She is said to have ransomed over a thousand
Jewish prisoners out of her own means. Immanuel
Aboab, the chronicler, who knew the family personally,
describes her in a passage that has become classical: "One
of the most noble and high-spirited matrons who have
existed in Israel since the time of our dispersion: such
was the Señora Benvenida Abrabanel — pattern of chas-
tity, of piety, of prudence and of valor." At the time of
Doña Gracia's arrival in Ferrara, she was past her prime
(she was to die in 1560) but still active; and the two
doubtless indulged in a friendly competition of well-
doing.

Nor were there lacking, at this time in Ferrara, Jewesses
who were of mark in a different sphere, though of lower
social status. This was the place of residence indeed of
the Modena family, which was memorable for the scholarly women which it produced, who in turn provided the
model and inspiration for a succession of famous rabbis.
At the time of Doña Gracia's arrival, there was still living
there, in all probability, Pomona Modena, the mother
of Abraham ben Daniel Modena, who had celebrated her
piety in his poems: she, we are informed, was versed in
the Talmud as well as any man, and Rabbi David of

Imola addressed her on one occasion a detailed responsum on a point of Jewish law, which only a scholar could have understood. Yet more famous was her kinswoman, Bathsheba (Fioretta), the wife of Solomon Modena and mother of the physician Mordecai Modena, and ancestress of a whole line of scholars, including Leone da Modena, pride and shame of the Venetian Ghetto in a later generation, and of Aaron Berechiah da Modena, one of the last of the inspired synagogue hymnologists. She, we are told by one of her grandchildren, was constantly engaged in study, had a considerable acquaintance even with the *Zohar*, was expert in the writings of Maimonides and had a regular sequence of study each week; and her influence in developing and in maintaining the love of Jewish learning in her family was gratefully recognized. Ultimately, as an old woman, she emigrated to Palestine, ending her days very shortly afterwards in the Holy City of Safed. At the time of Doña Gracia's arrival in Ferrara, she was as yet in her prime. It is not too much to suggest that she may have had some influence on the other's mental development and perhaps assisted to familiarize her with the Jewish background from which, owing to the circumstances of her life, she had hitherto been estranged.[5]

Of Doña Gracia's immediate circle, upon whom she relied heavily for advice in business and practical matters, the most noteworthy was of course her nephew, João Miguez, who visited Ferrara from time to time; the main seat of his activity, however, at this period seems to have been abroad, especially at Lyons. His brother, Samuel Nasi, the younger Gracia's husband, was apparently content with that position, playing throughout his life a

minor role. Another member of the family circle, though
less immediately related, was Agostino Enriques (known
secretly as Abraham Benveniste, though he had not yet
embraced Judaism in public) — an adroit man of affairs
who had been with her at Antwerp and whom Diogo
Mendes had nominated in his last will as co-guardian of
his daughter with Miguez should Doña Gracia die. As
her brother-in-law had advised, she took his advice in
every matter of importance. Ultimately it turned out
that he was basically dishonest, and it is probable that
he had been swindling her right along. Of an entirely
different type and vastly superior character was Duarte
Gomez, who belonged to the old Jewish family of Za-
boca — a graduate of the University of Salamanca,
where he had studied medicine, but now a business man
and the trusted agent of the firm. He had a strong literary
bent, translated Petrarch into Spanish verse in a masterly
fashion in the meter of the original, contributed laudatory
poems to works by other writers, patronized letters, and
was on terms of familiarity with many Italian littera-
teurs — a typical specimen of the highly-cultured Marrano magnate of the day.[6] At least twice in his lifetime,
he was arraigned by the Inquisition on the charge of
Judaizing, but on both occasions without result; though
after his death one at least of his sons returned to Judaism
and had to answer before the Holy Office for the posses-
sion of various heretical works from his father's library.

Of the less conspicuous members of the community we
are minutely informed in some cases, thanks to the depositions discovered in the Inquisitional archives at Lisbon
and elsewhere. Some of them were indeed old friends and
acquaintances from Antwerp, who had sought refuge in

Ferrara when their colony there had been disturbed.
Among the rank and file of the community perhaps the
most prominent was a young goldsmith named Abraham
Saralvo (formerly Gabriel Henriques) who exerted himself
to bring about the admission of fugitive Marranos (hundreds of them, it was said) to the Covenant of Abraham;
later on, he was to pay dearly for his devotion, being
burnt alive on the Campo de' Fiori in Rome in 1583.
Amatus Lusitanus was there too, occupying some sort of
position at the University, and once more in medical
attendance on the family. Nor can there be any doubt
that they were on familiar terms with the other notables
of the city and distinguished strangers who came there
from time to time — not only Jews: it is known at all
events that they entertained the French ambassador to
Venice on one occasion when he visited the inland
duchy.

The brilliant, tolerant, but not too exalted Court of
the Estensi was at this time at the height of its fame.
Jews were not strangers to it. (We know how in an earlier
generation a member of the local community had lost
3,000 ducats at a single sitting when playing cards with
the Duke!) It was natural therefore that, while Doña
Gracia immersed herself in her graver preoccupations,
the other members of the family had more worldly diver-
sions. Of this, one supremely interesting relic has survived. The Jews of Renaissance Italy had the same
tastes and interests as their neighbors, and some of them
had portrait-medals struck, in the spirit of the age. (We
know those of Benjamin, son of the physician Elijah
Beer, of 1503(?); of Elias and his mother Rica de Lattes, of
Rome, 1552; of Abraham Emanuel Norsa, most probably

of Mantua, 1557.) Gracia *la chica* followed suit, entrust-
ing the commission to the fashionable Ferrarese artist,
Pastorino de' Pastorini (1508–1572) who was also to be
responsible for the last of the three mentioned above.[7]
His production, showing the young lady at the age of
eighteen, is a delightful one. Her face is molded in profile,
facing right. She is dressed in the height of mid-sixteenth-
century fashion, like any noblewoman of the time —
décolleté bodice with a stiff, heavily-embroidered collar
supporting the back of the neck, pearls in her headdress
from which a cascade of veiling falls over her shoulders,
elaborate earrings and costly necklace. Her newly-
found Jewish pride is demonstrated in the fact that,
though her age is indicated in Latin (A. AE. xviii) her
name, Gracia Nasi, is given in exquisitely-engraved
Hebrew characters. The face is grave and beautiful,
though perhaps a little heavy. It is a delightful repre-
sentation of a Jewess of the upper class in Italy at the
heyday of the Renaissance, and among the most charm-
ing artistic relics of the period. Add a few years to the
features, and perhaps a few gems to the jewelry, and
you doubtless have Doña Gracia the elder, still not past
the prime of life.[8]

It was at this time that Gracia Nasi became known as
a patroness of letters. Just after her arrival (the two
phenomena are surely not unconnected) Ferrara began
a new tradition in Jewish literature, by first producing
works in the vernacular, for the benefit of recently-
arrived Marranos who were ignorant of Hebrew. The
lead was taken by a certain Yomtob Athias, known in
his Marrano days as Jeronimo de Vargas,[9] who in 1552
completed the production of the first published Spanish

version of the traditional prayer book (*Lybro de Oracyones de todo el año*: Ferrara, 1552). This proved to be the precursor of a notable series of such works.

The most important of them all was a translation of the Hebrew Bible ("The Ferrara Bible," it is generally called) produced in collaboration with a certain Abraham Usque or Duarte Pinel, probably at Doña Gracia's expense. (It was not in fact a new version, but the traditional word-for-word translation which had been current among the Spanish Jews for centuries, revised here and there in minor details.) There are certain incidental facts about this famous work — a noble folio, printed in black letter — which endow it with a dramatic interest. It was published in two editions, one for Jews and one for Christians. The most striking and obvious differences between the two are at the beginning and the end. Both forms, according to the title-page, were "seen and examined by the Office of the Inquisition," and both appeared "with the privilege of the most illustrious duke of Ferrara." The dedication following this, and the colophon at the close of the volume, are, however, strikingly different in the two issues. The one, intended for general use, or perhaps for export to the Peninsula, is dedicated to the duke of Ferrara, dated in accordance with Christian convention, and signed by those responsible with their Marrano names, Duarte Pinel and Jeronimo de Vargas; the other, intended for the Jews, gives the Jewish equivalents of these names, Abraham Usque and Yomtob Athias, bears the Hebrew date and is dedicated to the noble-hearted Jewess, Doña Gracia 'Naci.' (There is an incidental difference also in the text, some copies translating a famous passage of Isaiah

7.14, *"and the virgin,"* and some *"and the maiden* shall conceive and bear a child.")[10]

It is worth while to give here the dedication to the "Jewish" version, with all its characteristic sixteenth-century rhetoric, at length: —

Prologue to the Very Magnificent Lady: Doña Gracia Naci

It would not seem proper (most magnificent Lady) that, now we are about to print the Bible in our Spanish tongue (translated from the Hebrew word for word — so rare a work, never before known until our day) it should be offered to persons whose favor could not help it, but to one so noble and magnanimous, that it would adorn her nobility. Therefore we desired to direct it to Your Honor, as being a person whose merits have always earned the most sublime place among all of our people — both because your greatness deserves it, and because your own birth and love of your land imposes this well-deserved obligation upon us. We pray Your Honor to accept it with the good will wherewith we offer it, and to favor it and guard it with the same mind wherewith you have hitherto always favored all who thus far have obtained your help. And because your nobility is naturally accustomed to these offices, we are quieted of any misgiving we might have by reason of the diversity of opinions; begging you that your memory will not forget our desire, which is so profoundly inclined for your service. May our God guard your person and prosper your magnificent estate for very ample years.

The servants of Your Honor,
Yom Tob Atias and Abraham Usque.

[March 1, 1553]

Later in the same year another work appeared at Ferrara under similar auspices — one of the most notable in the record of vernacular Jewish literature. This was the famous *Consolaçam às Tribulaçoens de Israel,* or "Consolation for the Tribulations of Israel," by Samuel

Usque — no immediate relation so far as is known of
Abraham Usque, who published the volume for him in
1553. It is a prose-poem in Portuguese, in the form of a
pastoral dialogue between "Ycabo" (i. e., Ichabod: it is
also an anagram for Jacob), "Numeo" (i. e., Nahum, the
Comforter) and Zachariah (i. e., God's Remembrance),
which passes in review the whole of Israel's history, recalls
the unutterably long sequence of suffering and brings
together the divine promises of hope contained in the
Bible, with other arguments that should save the agonized Jew from despair. It was written, says the author
in his preface, for the express purpose of assisting the
crypto-Jews of Portugal and prevent them from being
overwhelmed by what they had undergone. The third
dialogue consists largely of a chronicle of Jewish martyrdom in Christian Europe, embodying much information
to be found in no other sources. It is a remarkable work,
written in a style of such exquisite beauty that it is today
regarded as a Portuguese classic and read in the Portuguese schools — a curious irony of history, considering
where and why it was composed.

This work also appeared under Doña Gracia's auspices
and was dedicated to her in moving terms: —

Since my first object is to serve with this little branch of new
fruit our Portuguese nation, it is proper to offer it to your
Excellence, as the heart of this body; because in the remedies
which you have given you have felt, and still feel, its travail
more than any other. I for my part cannot conceal that I am,
Illustrious Lady, your creature, whom I wish to serve with
works and writings and deeds so as to show my gratitude in
part for the many favors I have received from your hand. For,
ever since you began to show your light, even the least creatures
of this people began to babble this truth, in whose bones your
name and happy memory will be carved forever. . . .

The work was indeed a distinct success, and Doña Gracia's name was closely associated with it in the minds of readers. There is a curious illustration of this in an Inquisitional denunciation discovered not long since, from which we learn how, as early as 1554 — the year after its publication — it circulated in England, and was even copied by hand; the copy, it seemed, lacked its title page, and was entitled (so the deponent stated; it is probable that his recollection to some extent misled him) "To Beatriz de Luna, wife of Diogo Mendes."[11]

Meanwhile, Doña Gracia was continuing her great work on behalf of her fellow Marranos, helping them to escape from Portugal, asssisting them to transfer their property and enabling them to settle in the ever-open haven of Turkey or, under her own aegis, in Ferrara. It was with this work especially that her grateful contemporaries associated her. In the dedication to the *Consolation for the Tribulations of Israel*, Samuel Usque lauded in unmeasured terms "what you have done and still do to bring to the light the fruits of those plants that are buried there [in Portugal] in darkness." This is amplified towards the close of the work in the memorable passage in which "Numeo," the consoler, enumerates the many manifestations of Divine Providence that had saved the Jewish people from disaster in the recent period of stress and oppression. One entire section of this is devoted to Doña Gracia's work in organizing the flight of the refugees from Portugal. No exact details are given, but the language used conveys some idea of her devotion, her unremitting energy and the scale of her work, not hitherto appreciated to the full. There is no such panegyric to a woman in the whole of Jewish literature:

Nor should you forget the help which you have had in the trav-
ails which (as you say) you have experienced on the road from
Portugal until you arrived in safety. Who has seen, as you
have, the Divine mercy reveal itself in human guise, as He has
shown and continues to show you for your succor? Who
has seen revived the intrinsic piety of Miriam, offering her life
to save her brethren? the great prudence of Deborah, in gov-
erning her people? that infinite virtue and great sanctity of
Esther, in helping those who are persecuted? the much praised
strength of the most chaste and magnanimous widow Judith,
in delivering those hemmed in by travail? Such has the Lord
sent to you in these days from the most supreme rank of His
armies, embodying them in a soul of His which by high chance
and your happy lot is installed in the most proper womanly
body of the fortunate Jewess Nasci.[12] She it is who at the
beginning of their journey greatly helps your necessitous sons,
who are prevented by penury from saving themselves from the
pyre and undertaking so long a road, her hope giving them
strength. As for those who have already left and have arrived
in Flanders and elsewhere overcome by poverty, or who stand
distressed by the sea in danger that they will not be able to
fare further, she helps these her dependents with a most liberal
hand, with money and many other aids and comforts. It is she
who shows them favor in the asperity of the stormy Alps of
Germany and in other lands, and in the extreme misery when
the many horrors and misfortunes of the long voyage overtake
them, helping them willingly with her succor. It is she who
aided you with motherly love and heavenly liberality in the
dangerous and urgent necessities which you experienced in
the unexpected exile from that Italian city [which you know] —[13]
providing for all the magnates in a time when they coud not
help themselves out of their own means; succoring the multi-
tude of necessitous and miserable poor, refusing no favor even
to those who were her enemies and [sending] boatloads of bread
and necessities to all, in such wise that she almost revived them
from the grave which threatened them in those waters. In
such wise, with her golden arm and heavenly grasp, she raised
most of those of this people from the depths of this and other
infinite travail in which they were kept enthralled in Europe
by poverty and sin; she brings them to safe lands and does not
cease to guide them, and gathers them to the obedience and
precepts of their God of old. Thus she has been your tried
strength in your weakness; a bank where the weary rest; a
fountain of clear water where the parched drink; a fruit-laden
shady tree where the hungry eat and the desolate find rest;

and for you, more particularly, she was part of that great succor, and remains at all times a tried relief in all the miseries
of the Portuguese people — a strong column to support many
who were once prosperous and to help them with her own
fortune. In brief, the wide pinions and outspread wings of
this eagle have saved a great part of your sons in their flight
from the cruelty of the Portuguese, so that she thus imitated
the Lord at the time of the Exodus from Egypt.

That is all we know. An infinity of suffering, of charity,
of adventure, of organization, seems to be suggested by
this passage; but the details, even then familiar to few,
are irrecoverable today. One can only imagine the great
house at Ferrara, and the constant coming and going of
envoys bearing new terrible accounts of the ravages of
the Inquisition and messages from those who were anxious to escape, and the consternation of the charitable
lady who received them. It is more difficult to reconstruct
in one's mind the full picture of the elaborate organization — the agencies maintained in Portugal itself to
coordinate plans, the observers in England, Flanders,
France and Germany who assisted the fugitives — all
perhaps agents of the Mendes banking-house — the
elaborate arrangements for directing them from stage to
stage and transmitting their money, and finally the
arrival in Ferrara and the immediate visit to the Nasi
mansion to pour out a thanks-laden heart before Doña
Gracia herself. It seems obvious from the almost hy-
perbolical terms of the passage quoted that one of the
beneficiaries who owed his escape to her was the author,
Samuel Usque himself.[14]

Against all expectation, she had to extend her relief
work even to her place of refuge — "the most secure
haven of Italy," as Usque called it. In 1551, not long

TITLE PAGE OF A BOOK SHOWING THE USQUE
PRINTER'S MARK

Prologo a la muy magnifica Señora
doña Gracia Naci.

O parescia razon (muy magnifica Señora) que auiendose de ympri
mir la Biblia en nuestra lengua Española (traduzida del Hebreo pa,
labra por palabra obra tan rara y hasta nuestros tiempos nunca vista)
fuesse a parar en personas de cuyo fauor no se pudiesse valer sino a al
guna tan noble y magnanima que a su nobleza acrecentasse ornamien
to. Por la qual causa la quesimos dirigir a vuestra merced como a persona que sus
meritos entre todos los nuestros siempre tuuieron el mas sublime lugar: assi por sus
grandezas lo merescer como por que la propria naturaleza y amor dela patria nos
pone esta obligacion tan deuida: vuestra merced la acepte con la voluntad que nos
se la offrecemos y la fauoresca y defienda conel animo que siempre fauorescio to
dos los que su ayuda hasta oy ympetraron. Y por que su nobleza naturalmente es
acostumbrada a estos officios quedamos seguros de algun recelo que por la diuer
sidad de juizios podriamos tener: pidiendo que su memoria no se oluide de nue
stro desseo que tan ynclinado es a su seruicio. Nuestro Señor por muy largos
años guarde su persona y prospere su magnifico estado.

Seruidores de vuestra merced.

Yom Tob Atias y Abraham Usque.

THE PROLOGUE DEDICATION OF YOM TOB ATIAS
AND ABRAHAM USQUE TO DONA GRACIA

after her arrival, there was an outbreak of plague in the
city, the infection having been brought, according to
the general opinion, from Germany and Switzerland.
Who should have carried it, men asked, but the Marranos who travelled that way on their devious journey
from Portugal? As the plague spread, so the anti-alien
agitation grew, until the duke was compelled in spite of
himself to order the newly-arrived Portuguese to leave
the city — not because of fanaticism, for once, but as a
purely sanitary measure. Their sufferings were increased
by the fact that the timorous population, fearing infection, would not enter into any sort of contact with them
meanwhile for any price. The time-limit expired at night;
and in the darkness old men tottered down the roads,
carrying everything they possessed, so as to cross the
boundary in time. On the river-bank, where boats awaited
them, many of them were despoiled by the men-at-arms
sent to protect them. Later on, several lost their lives
as they wandered from place to place in Italy, or were
assailed on the high seas on their way to the Levant.
Great as the disaster was for them, it would have been
greater still but for the singlehearted devotion of Doña
Gracia, who organized their movements, helped them
with supplies and money, and despatched up the river
boats laden with food to relieve their immediate distress.
However, in due course the scare died down and the exiles
were allowed to return to the city, the Marrano community now attaining its greatest prosperity.

It seems that Doña Gracia herself had been among those
who were compelled to leave Ferrara as a result of the
scare: for there is no other reasonable explanation of the
fact that, just at this period, we find her in Venice again.[15]

We happen to know that while she was there in this year she purchased from the viceroy of India a rare gem, believed to have medicinal properties and to be an antidote against poison, which cost her as much as one hundred and thirty ducats.[16] It was unwise to venture into the very lion's mouth — even that of the bookish lion of St. Mark — so shortly after her recent misadventures and escapes, while the edict of expulsion of the Marranos was so fresh in the public recollection and everyone was well aware that she had so recently made public profession of her Judaism. There is reason to believe that she was again arrested — presumably this time on the well-grounded charge of apostasy from Christianity — or at least submitted to cavalier treatment. The news was soon reported in Constantinople where the interest of the sultan was again enlisted. (It was believed that Dr. Moses Hamon, the imperial body-physician, still anxious for a marriage alliance between the two families, was again, as on a previous occasion, the principal intermediary.) Once more, a Court messenger was sent to Venice to make representations. His report of the manner in which Doña Gracia had been treated threw the Grand Signior and his ministers into a fury. A minor diplomatic crisis ensued. There was consternation among the European observers at the Sublime Porte. The Venetian *bailo* journeyed especially to Adrianople after the Court in order to calm the troubled waters, but without success, and his despatches home dealt with the matter as being one of primary international importance.[17] Once again, Doña Gracia escaped unscathed, returning in due course to Ferrara, where the panic had by now subsided; but the experience forced her to reconsider her position.

The Italian sky was rapidly clouding over. Cardinal Caraffa was now all-powerful at the papal Court, and the Counter-Reformation had begun. The Jesuit Order had been founded, the Inquisition had been reorganized, a propaganda for securing the conversion of the Jews had been set in motion, a coterie of apostates was carrying on a whispering campaign in Rome, with results that were to prove extremely serious before long, and the grand assault on Hebrew literature was in preparation. To persons compelled to think ahead of events, and with special sources of information, the anti-Jewish reaction which was to culminate so drastically a year or so later was already tragically obvious. Christian Europe, its skies darkened by the smoke from the Inquisitional pyres, was no environment for former Marranos, who might at any moment be pounced upon and prosecuted if the tolerant whim of the temporal ruler changed, or another person acceded to authority. Only Turkey held out the prospect of unbroken tranquility. Already a great part of the family property had been transferred thither, thanks to the warm benevolence of the Sublime Porte, more and more anxious to acquire these fresh valuable subjects and to become the seat of the activities of one of the greatest of European business houses. The requisite safe-conduct had long since been obtained, while further arrangements were made with the states, large and small, through which the immigrants had to pass on their journey. All the difficulties were at last overcome. In August, 1552, Doña Gracia left Ferrara, with her family and an enormous retinue, her face set towards Turkey.

GENEALOGICAL TREE

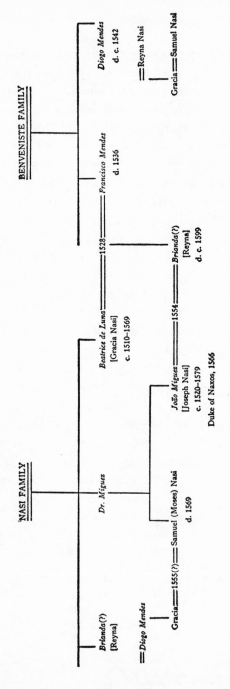

Marrano names are in italics; Jewish names in brackets.
Marriages are indicated by a double line.
Year of death is preceded by the letter d.

CHAPTER V

Constantinople

IT WAS in the spring of the year of the Creation 5313, of Grace 1553, and of the Hejira 961, that Doña Beatrice de Luna, now Gracia Nasi, arrived in Constantinople. It was almost a state entry. Four roomy coaches, so magnificent that observers spoke of them as "triumphal chariots," bore the ladies of the party, with their own companions and serving-wenches, all richly dressed. Around them rode an escort of forty armed men, who had ensured their safety in the hazardous journey across the Balkans. In the foremost vehicle sat Doña Gracia — at last, in her forty-fourth year, reaching the end of her long odyssey, triumphant over her enemies. With her was her daughter Reyna. Her errant sister had not yet arrived, although expected, while Don Samuel and his bride had been left behind at Ferrara, and João Miguez was still looking after the family business interests in the various European commercial centers.

The Jews of Constantinople swarmed excitedly around the procession as it entered, already aware of the identity of the new arrivals and of what Doña Gracia (whose reputation had preceded her) had done in the past for her people. It was a gala day for them as well; for the happy escape and safe arrival were celebrated by the distribution of thousands of ducats to the poor and the public hospitals and communal charities. The foreign colony in the city looked on with an admixture of bewilderment and contempt; and the Spanish litterateur Andrés Laguna (then a prisoner of war in Turkey, and posing as a physician) considered the episode of sufficient importance to be recorded in his reminiscences:[1] –

One day a Portuguese lady who called herself Doña Beatriz Mendes, who was very rich, entered Constantinople with forty horsemen and four triumphal chariots filled with Spanish ladies and serving-women. The household that she had with her was not less than that of a Spanish duke; and she could afford it, for she is very rich. She had her respects paid for her at Court. She had arranged with the Grand Turk, while she was still living in Venice, that she did not require any special privilege in his territories, except that her household need not wear clothes like those of the other Jews, but stomachers and coifs in the Venetian style. This she obtained — and would have obtained more too if she had desired it, to have such a subject.... In a trice, you could now see this Señora Doña Beatriz change her name and call herself Doña Gracia de Luna *et tota Hierosolima cum illa* ["and all Jerusalem with her"].

This may be supplemented from the reminiscences of the German, Hans Dernschwam, the factor of the Fugger banking house, who also happened to be in Constantinople at the time:–

In 1553 an old(!) Portuguese woman came from Venice to Constantinople, with her daughter and attendants. The Jews are not in agreement as to who her husband was and what his name was; some say that he was called Diego Me[n]des and his brother was Francisco de Anversa [i. e., of Antwerp]. She is reported to have escaped with great wealth from Portugal to Venice after her husband's death; she is said to have a sister there who was supposed to come here, but has somehow been detained. The Jews are very proud of her and call her *Señora*. She lives also in luxury and extravagance; has many servants, serving-wenches also, among them two from the Netherlands. She is said to have been formerly a Marrano and to have become a Jewess again. . . .

The Venetians are reported to have arrested her and to have refused to let her go. She is then said to have intrigued with the sultan's physician, who had a son and hoped she would give him her daughter. The sultan is then supposed to have taken the part of the *Señora* and they had to let her go from Venice. . . . They allege that they have left a lot of wealth behind them; also that some is following them by sea. Considering the cost of living in Turkey, their wealth will soon shrink here. They gave the pashas a lot, and distributed several thousand ducats to the poor Jews and their hospital. . . .[2]

These passages, with all their exaggeration and petty malice, show at least what intense interest was aroused in all circles in Constantinople by the family's arrival.

The journey from Italy had been slow and leisurely. Avoiding Venice for obvious reasons, they had gone probably by land from Ferrara to Ancona; here they would have found a numerous settlement of Marrano refugees from Portugal confiding in the papal protection and oblivious of the terrible fate that was in store for them.[3] Hence they would have taken ship across the Adriatic to the city-republic of Ragusa (now called Dubrovnik) — a miniature Venice, beautifully situated on an inlet of the sea. Here they arrived at the beginning of 1553, being received with great ceremony by the government. In the previous November, Doña Gracia had presented a petition to it through her local agents, Abner Alfarin and Isaac Ergas, requesting a special arrangement to facilitate the payment of the customs-duties on the merchandise she proposed to send through that port. In view of the great sums of money that would be involved, she asked to be allowed six months for settlement, for which she was, of course, prepared to give adequate sureties; she wished to hire a warehouse in the harbor area for the accommodation of her property in transit,

which was to be immune from confiscation on any pretext whatsoever; and there was to be no additional duty
payable on goods which she re-exported. This agreement
was to be valid for five years. In return for these concessions she was prepared to pay 500 ducats in advance,
which sum was not to be refunded to her even if no use
were made of the facilities granted. Moreover, her agents
promised to induce their correspondents and friends to
transmit their merchandise, too, by the same route,
to the manifest advantage of the Ragusan republic. It
is obvious from the phraseology and the conditions what
a vast amount of property was involved in this transference. Doña Gracia's cordial reception when she passed
through the city, for which she subsequently expressed her
profound appreciation, is thus easily to be understood.[4]

The safest and probably the most pleasant way thence
towards her goal was overland, across the Balkans, along
the line of the old Roman road, the *Via Egnatia*. The
next important city on their way was Salonica, now at
the height of its amazing expansion. It was a microcosm
of the entire Jewish world. There were Jews from France,
Italy, Germany, Hungary, Calabria, Apulia, Sicily and
every province of Spain, each group maintaining its own
synagogue and congregation. Every ship that arrived
from the West and every mule-train that came from the
north brought a fresh contingent of Portuguese Marranos. Jews constituted the majority of the population,
as continued to be the case until very recent times.
(During the course of the German occupation of 1941–4,
this great Jewish center, with all its superb historical
tradition, was all but exterminated — one of the greatest tragedies of even that tragic era.) They not only

controlled trade and industry, but furnished also the artisans, the fishermen, the stevedores and the harbor-workers; and, as continued to be the case down to our own generation, no ship could unload in the port on the Sabbath. The fashions, the habits, the dishes, the languages, the costumes, even the lullabies of Toledo and Seville, as they had existed at the close of the previous century, were incongruously perpetuated in the framework of classical monuments and under the supercilious eyes of Turkish janissaries. Every synagogue, of course, had its academy attached to it, so that the city was now one of the greatest seats of rabbinic learning in the world. There were scholars of a different type too — physicians educated at Salamanca or Coimbra, patricians whose libraries would not have discredited Saragossa, philosophers who would have been at home in Florence or Naples. It would have been a congenial environment for Doña Gracia to have dallied or even settled in, and we may be sure that she visited, watched, observed, admired, perhaps berated, and distributed lavish though discriminating charity.

But her goal was farther on, and the sultan would not perhaps have approved her settling in this provincial center of his empire. Not long thereafter she made her impressive entry into the capital.

It was an amazing new world into which the storm-tossed convoy of refugees arrived. Just over a century before, the forces of the Crescent under Mohammed the Conqueror had forced an entry into Constantinople through the unguarded Romanos Postern. The Roman Emperor Constantine XIII, last successor of Constantine the Great, had been inconsequentially killed in the fighting which followed; and with him the Byzantine empire fell, after a thousand gaudy years. The Moslem domination in the Near East was thenceforth unchallengeable; and where the involved ceremonial of the Greek court had hitherto dazzled and intimidated observers, the Turks now staged their clumsy imitations. By the side of the ancient Church of the Holy Wisdom or *Hagia Sophia* (of course transformed into a mosque, with its glowing mosaics covered over with layers of whitewash), the conqueror constructed his sprawling palaces, the Old Serai and the New Serai, and austere places of worship with delicate minarets, from which the muezzins could summon the faithful to prayer. But more than this was needed to create a capital. A population over-civilized beyond the point of effeteness had been overwhelmed by newcomers still on the verge of barbarism and efficient only in the military sphere. After the three days of unbridled pillage on the latter's part were over, the sultan showed that he realized how absurd it would be to use only them to repopulate the imperial city. As had already been the case in the provincial centers, he had to fall back on the service of unbelievers. Christians were encouraged to take up their residence again in the city, being accorded a considerable degree of civil as well as of religious autonomy under the Patriarchs of the respective sects, Greek and Armenian, who enjoyed great state and authority. But clearly, from the point of view of the Turks, the Jews constituted a far more valuable and far more reliable element, for there could be with them no question of faltering or conditional allegiance. Accordingly they, too, were specifically invited to return to their old homes, to reopen their synagogues and schools and to resume their former activities. Elijah Capsali, member of an ancient and renowned family from the island of Candia (Crete), was now nominated *Haham Bashi* or Chief Rabbi, being given a seat on the Imperial Divan next to the Mufti, and (such a thing had never been known to history before) with precedence over the Greek Patriarch.

The importance of the Jews of the empire at this time, in the third quarter of the fifteenth century, was relatively slight; for they had declined both numerically and intellectually under the blight of Byzantine intolerance. But the news of the changed circumstances spread rapidly to the utmost ends of the Diaspora. Even before the fall of Constantinople, an enthusiastic immigrant, newly-arrived in Turkey, sent a circular letter to the French and German communities, calling upon them to shake from their feet the dust of the cities of persecution and to emigrate with one accord to this new land of opportunity — not the least of the advantages of which was that it lay on the route to Palestine, the ultimate goal of every Jew's hopes and dreams. The reports of the last campaign against Constantinople were followed throughout the Jewish world with rapt attention; for it seemed to be the veritable War of Gog and Magog which was to usher in the Messianic deliverance. Thereafter, the immigration increased, every new arrival attracting more and more to follow him. With the expulsion from Spain in 1492, the settlement received a tremendous impetus. The Christian world, true to its record rather than its name, was with rare exceptions closed to the refugees. Only the Moslem world was open. To Africa, the unbelievers were admitted; to Turkey, they were avidly welcomed. The reason for this was plain: they provided precisely that element which was most necessary to the ill-balanced state — a class of city-dwellers, merchants and craftsmen, who could practice the handicrafts that the Turks so painfully lacked and, moreover, prevent commerce from being entirely in the hands of those whose interests were specifically anti-Turkish. "How can you call this Ferdinand 'wise' — he who has impoverished his dominions in order to enrich mine?" the reigning sultan, Bajazet II, is reported to have said with reference to His Catholic Majesty of Spain; and he welcomed the refugees with open arms. When, in 1550, the handful of Jews left in Provence were threatened with expulsion and sent a deputation to the Levant to find a place of refuge, their compatriots wrote them an ecstatic letter describing in dithyrambic terms the amplitude of their life in that generous land. The wealthy could find lucrative outlet for their capital, the poor dignified employment, and all kindly treatment and complete freedom from physical attack and unjust accusations. "We have no words," they concluded, "to record the enlargement and deliverance that has been achieved by the Jews in this place."

Thus encouraged, more immigrants came and more, by every vessel that arived from Western Europe. They settled by the score, the hundred, the thousand, in all the principal cities of the empire. They brought with them handicrafts and manufactures. They introduced the technical processes of the manufacture of firearms, gunpowder and cannon, which were used in battle against the improvident rulers who had driven them out; and unwonted activity among the blacksmiths and the iron-foundries in the Jewish quarter was taken as a sign that the Grand Turk meditated a new military foray. They continued the professions of goldsmith, which they had practiced with such outstanding success in the Peninsula, and widely introduced the textile and dyeing industries in which they traditionally had such great ability. In many places, glass-making and even metal-working were Jewish monopolies. (Near Salonica, at a place called Sidroscapsi, there was a community almost entirely engaged in gold and silver mining.) With their knowledge of foreign languages and conditions, they were the greatest competitors of the Venetians in the import and export trade, notwithstanding the latter's strong political backing; and no foreign merchant could dispense with their services as interpreters. Jewish physicians from the school of Salamanca, or those brought up in the great tradition of Hispano-Arabic medicine, were generally sought after for their discretion as well as their skill, being employed in the service of the sultan, the imperial harem, the grand viziers, and even foreign embassies, not unwilling to forget at so great a distance from home the Church's prohibition of the employment of infidels in this capacity. In brief, just as the persecutions under the Cross reached their climax, a dazzling new world was opened up under the silvery radiance of the Crescent. The poet-chronicler Samuel Usque compared the country to the Red Sea, which the Lord divided for His people, when they went forth from Egypt, drowning their troubles in its broad expanse.

Thus from the close of the fifteenth century, the history of the Jews in the Ottoman empire entered upon a new phase. The old indigenous communities, speaking Greek as their native language and following the Byzan-

tine rite in their prayers, were utterly submerged by the
immigrants from the fanaticism of Christian Europe.
Everywhere, new Spanish-speaking communities were
founded, or fresh synagogues following the *Sephardi* rite
came into existence by the side of the older ones. Brusa,
Angora, Smyrna, Magnesia, Nicopolis, Amasia all had
important settlements. At Adrianople, a contemporary
French traveller informs us, the Jews owned most of the
6,000 houses which the city boasted. But it was above
all the capital, together with the port of Salonica, which
especially attracted the exiles, their Jewish population
being raised to a level unparalleled hitherto in the history of the Diaspora — at all events since classical days.
The number of synagogues in Constantinople rose ultimately to 44; at Salonica it was almost as high. Little
groups who hailed from the same place clung together
in their new home, doing their best to preserve in their
social life and synagogal practice every trivial reminis-
cence of the old. New immigrants from Catalonia, from
Aragon, from Castille, from Apulia, from southern
France, from Italy, from Calabria, from Portugal, from
Sicily, could find a place of worship maintained by their
former compatriots, where the environment and the
dialect and the ritual would be familiar down to the last
minute detail. More than this: there were even synagogues formed by the exiles from individual towns, such
as Messina, Cordova or Granada. (In Salonica, with
its Lisbon and Coimbra and Syracuse and Evora synagogues, the communal mosaic was even more varied.)
Among themselves, the exiles spoke at first their former
languages with Babel-like consequences. In the long run,
however, Castilian, the tongue of the greatest single

nucleus, became predominant, though modified to a considerable extent by other dialects and absorbing certain
elements from all of them as well as from Hebrew and
Turkish. Such was in fact the cultural predominance of
the Spanish Jews that the natives, too, had to learn their
tongue, the Greek or other languages which they had
originally spoken being forgotten; and it was curious to
meet with "Griegos," living in a Greek-speaking environment and still preserving the Byzantine rite of prayer,
who had discarded their ancestral language in favor of
one spoken in the natural course of events fifteen hundred miles away. (An incidental result of the change was
that the unity of the former Byzantine Jewry was shattered, so that after the death in 1525 of Rabbi Elijah
Mizrahi, Capsali's successor, the office of *Haham Bashi*
was allowed to lapse, not being revived until the nineteenth century.) The catholic, all-embracing cultural
interests of the former Spanish Jewry, already going back
for half a millenium, were maintained, or renewed, under
distant skies. Many poets continued to employ the old
stately Hispanic meters, and at Constantinople there was
a Poetical Academy, an institution almost unique in the
history of the Diaspora. One scholar was to translate
from the Latin into Hebrew the prophecies of Michael de
Nostradamus (probably unaware that he was of Jewish
origin), and another from the Spanish the exploits of
Amadis de Gaul; while a third rendered the poetical
books of the Bible into Greek, and a fourth turned Leone
Ebreo's *Dialogues of Love* from Italian into Spanish.
That, at about the period of Doña Gracia's arrival, one
of the sultan's Jewish physicians (probably Moses Hamon)
was a keen collector of ancient manuscripts, even in

Greek (according to the humanist Busbecq, who was
acting as Imperial envoy in Constantinople at the time)
was completely in keeping with the environment.

There is an exceptionally graphic picture of Turkish
Jewry at this period in the reminiscences of a German
visitor named Hans Dernschwam — an employee of the
Fugger banking house, typical of his nation as much in
his powers of observation as in his anti-Jewish bias, who
travelled through Turkey just at the time of Doña
Gracia's arrival (1553–1555) and (as has been seen above)
specifically mentions her too in his travel-diary. It is
worth while to cite it at some length:[5]—

In Turkey you will find in every town innumerable Jews of all
countries and languages. And every Jewish group sticks together in accordance with its language. Wherever Jews have
been expelled in any land they all come together in Turkey, as
thick as vermin; speak German, Italian, Spanish, Portuguese,
French, Czechish, Polish, Greek, Turkish, Syriac, Chaldean
and other languages besides these. As is their custom, every
one wears clothes in accordance with the language he speaks.
Usually the garments are long, just like those of the Wal-
lachians, the Turks and the Greeks, too — that is, a caftan.
This is a long tunic, tied about at the waist, over which is a
sort of skirt made of cloth of good quality and silk. Just as the
Turks wear white turbans, the Jews wear yellow. Some foreign
Jews still wear the black Italian birettas [square caps]. Some
who pretend to be physicians or surgeons wear the red, pointed,
elongated birettas.

In Constantinople, the Jews are thick as ants. The Jews
themselves say that they are very numerous. However, in the
tax list of the past year of 1553, there are supposed to have
been 15,035 Jews, not counting women and children, and
6,785 Christians, such as Greeks, Armenians, Caramanians, all
of whom pay the sultan the tax called the *Kharadj*. The Jews
are despised in Turkey as they are anywhere else; possess no
estates, although many own their own homes.

In those places where they can find shelter and have their
own quarters or a place to make a living, they prefer to live in
the houses of others and pay rent. Most of these houses belong

to the mosques or to the priests. When the houses burn down, the Moslem priests have to build them again. They live in the lower part of the city near the sea. Not far from Adrianople is a city on the Aegean called Salonica. It is believed that more Jews live there than in Constantinople — they say, about 20,000. Many are cloth-weavers, whose products are sold throughout Turkey....

In Alexandria, in Missr (that is to say, Cairo), in Aleppo, in Antioch in Syria, and in Jerusalem and everywhere else, there are many Jews. Those Jews that are old, who have a little money, travel to the Holy Land, to Jerusalem, and still hope that they will one day all come together, from all countries, into their own native land and there secure hold of the government. The well-to-do Jews send money to Jerusalem to support them, for one cannot make any money there, nor is there any money there.... There are forty-two or more synagogues in Constantinople. Every Jewish nationality goes to its own synagogue.

The Jews lend nothing to the Turks. The latter are not to be trusted. The Jews are allowed to travel and to do business anywhere they wish in Turkey, Egypt, Missr (that is, Cairo), Alexandria, Aleppo, Armenia, Tataria, Babylonia as far as Persia, Reussen, Poland and Hungary. There is no spot in the world which hasn't some of its Jews in Constantinople and there are no wares which the Jews do not carry about and trade in. Just as soon as a foreign ship comes in from Alexandria, Kaffa, Venice and other places, the Jews are the first to clamber over the side. They import all the jewels that come to Constantinople from India by way of Persia ...

Many Marranos — that is Jews who turned Christian, as in Spain, or voluntarily became Christians in other places —... all come to Turkey and become Jews again. They endure contempt, poverty, hunger, thirst, in order to be able to have time for themselves and not be kept captive by the Turks like the Christians. About the year 1552, before we entered Turkey, a scholarly German died at Constantinople. He knew both Greek and Arabic, got in among the Jews and accepted their faith. He also learned Hebrew. The Jews boast that many Christians come into the country every year and become Jews.....

There are all sorts of artisans among the Jews who make a living selling their products publicly, for in Turkey every man is free to carry on his trade at home, in a shop or on the streets. Whether he is skilled or not, knows little or much, no one has a

word to say if he only pays his tax to the sultan and his rent
for the shop. . . .

There are two cloth-shearers among the Jews and some
among the Greeks too. The Jews of Constantinople also have
a printing press and print many rare books. They have gold-
smiths, lapidaries, painters, tailors, butchers, druggists, physicians, surgeons, cloth-weavers, wound-surgeons, barbers, mir-
ror-makers, dyers . . . silk-workers, gold-washers, refiners of ores,
assayers, engravers. . . .

The sultan has never used any but a certain Jewish physician,
who probably rendered good service to him and the Court. He
was allowed to build a large stone house of three or four stories
in the Jewish quarter. He died while we were at Constantinople.
His son also said to be a physician. He now has his father's
position; is said to have a prescription to cure a bellyache.[6]
The Jews also have a few druggists. . . .

The Jews do not allow any of their own to go about begging.
They have collectors who go from house to house and collect into
a common chest for the poor. This is used to support the poor
and the hospital.

Nicolas de Nicolay, Seigneur d'Arfeville, Chamberlain
and Geographer in Ordinary to the King of France, who
accompanied the French ambassador to Constantinople
about this period, may be presumed to have met Doña
Gracia and her family, though he does not record the
fact. On the other hand, like other occidental tourists
of the time, he devotes a good deal of attention to the
Jews in his famous work *Navigations, Peregrinations et
voyages faicts en la Turquie*. The quantity of those living
in Turkey, and especially in Constantinople, was to his
mind "marvellous, and almost incredible." Their numbers and business activity increased, he said, almost
daily, with the result that[7]

At the present day they have in their hands the most and
greatest traffic of merchandise and ready money that is in the
Levant. And likewise the shops and warehouses, the best
furnished with all rich sorts of merchandises, which are in

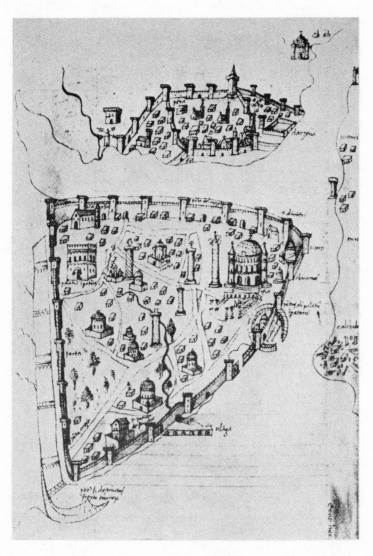

A Map of Constantinople

from a manuscript

Medicin Iuif.

A Turkish Jewish Physician

Constantinople, are those of the Jews. Likewise, they have amongst them workmen of all arts and handicrafts most excellent, and especially of the *Maranes*, of late banished and driven out of Spain and Portugal, who, to the great detriment and damage of Christianity, have taught the Turks divers inventions, crafts and engines of war, as to make artillery, harquebuses, gunpowder, shot and other ammunition; they have also there set up printing, not before seen in those countries. . . .

Like other observers who visited the country at this time, he was greatly impressed by the number of Jewish physicians in Constantinople (easily recognizable by their tall scarlet headgear) who, he said, easily outnumbered the Turks. Many of them he considered to be learned in theory as well as skilled in practice, largely because of their knowledge of foreign languages (such as Greek, Arabic, Chaldee and Hebrew), which rendered them better able to study than their competitors. He spoke with particular respect of Moses Hamon, Doña Gracia's friend and former protector, whose name recurs time after time in the records of the period.

There was, as a matter of fact, another side to the picture of unmitigated well-being: for the general impression, that the lot of the immigrants into Turkey in the fifteenth and sixteenth centuries left nothing whatsoever to be desired, is far more roseate than the facts warrant. Though the Jews of the Ottoman empire at this time had the unusual experience of finding themselves on a footing of equality with Christians, they were constantly reminded of their inferiority to Moslems. Like all *rayas* or unbelievers, they had to pay special taxation, which sometimes was of almost crushing weight (no fewer than seventeen different imposts are recorded at this period); and one of the main functions of the *ketkhuda* or *kahiya*,

the man-of-affairs who from now onwards represented
the community regularly at Court, was not to defend
them against injustice and oppression, as is usually stated,
but to supervise the partition and exaction of these levies.
Though there was no impediment worth mentioning on
the choice of occupation, as there was throughout Christian Europe, various contemptuous restrictions of other
sorts were enforced, and there were some incidental regu-
lations of a most galling nature. They had to submit, too,
to numerous minor indignities at Moslem hands. Public
security left a good deal to be desired, and long centuries
afterwards Jewish mothers continued to invoke the name
of the janissaries to frighten disobedient children. (An
English traveller of the next generation, the poet George
Sandys, remarking on the frequent fires in Constantinople, goes so far as to suggest that the Aga and his
janissaries "not seldome ... themselves set the Jews'
houses on fire,[8] who, made wary by the example, are now
furnished of arched vaults for the safeguard of their goods,
which are not to be violated by the flame.")[8a] Many of
the Imperial ministers, especially those who were of
Christian origin, looked askance upon the Jews; indeed,
it was said that not many years since, in 1536, they had
escaped a thorough-going persecution in the occidental
sense at the hands of the then grand vizier, Ibrahim
Pasha, a Greek renegade, only because of his sudden dis-
grace and execution on a suspicion of treachery. The
ground was in fact fully prepared for reaction. This, to
be sure, was not to take place until another full generation had passed, nor was it ever to be as sweeping as in
Christian Europe, or even to approach this standard
remotely. For the moment, Turkey was in the eyes of

the downtrodden Jews throughout the world, in both the literal and the figurative senses, the vestibule and gateway to the Promised Land.

The Turkish sovereign at the time with which we are dealing was Suleiman I, dubbed by the Turks "the Lawgiver" and by his European contemporaries and their posterity "the Magnificent" — the most fortunate, though certainly not the greatest, of Turkish rulers. Well above middle height, spare and swarthy, he had in his face, according to the Venetian envoy (hardly likely to flatter, on this occasion at least), a remarkable dignity, which made him universally revered. Though now barely more than sixty, he had already been on the throne for upwards of thirty years, having succeeded his father, Selim I, at the age of twenty-six, in 1520. He combined in himself many of the qualities most useful in a sovereign, in particular that of being able to select and be guided by the ablest servants and advisers. It was true that he sometimes chose less wisely, tending to be overinfluenced by unscrupulous ministers or the momentary favorite of his harem, henceforth a power to be reckoned with in the Ottoman state; but his blunders were few, and were generally redeemed by his sound sense of balance and his almost invariable good fortune in public though not in private affairs. He had inherited a full treasury, an orderly state and an undefeated army. In a series of brilliant though extravagant campaigns he added to his dominions wide territories from Algiers in the west to Aden in the east, and including the greater part of the kingdom of Hungary and the islands of the Archipelago; and Turkey was now at the height of her power, though (as events were to prove) too exhausted to maintain it.

At home he doubled the revenues (though as the result
of crushing taxation), reformed the administration and
purged the army. He was a great builder, adorning his
new capital with a number of new public buildings and
mosques, which did much to establish outwardly its
oriental character, besides improving roads throughout
the empire, constructing bridges and safeguarding the
water supply by fresh aqueducts. Though devout, he
was tolerant, as shown by his alliance with France and
his amelioration of the lot of his non-Moslem subjects.
This same broadmindedness was reflected particularly
in his policy towards the Jews, and it was in his reign that
the communities of the Turkish empire attained the
zenith of their prosperity. More than once he intervened
to suppress the accusations of ritual murder, brought up
from time to time by irrepressible Greeks, and in the end
ordered that all such allegations should in future be tried
before the sultan himself. From his earliest days, he had
a Jew — generally of the Hamon family — as his body-
physician.

This innate tolerance, coupled with a shrewd sense of
statecraft, had prompted him, long before the Nasi
family came to Turkey, to demonstrate the utmost
benevolence towards them and to treat them as though
their intention of living under his rule made them Turkish-
protected subjects. Twice, as we have seen, he had
intervened at Venice on their behalf, when their prospects
seemed peculiarly black. Everything that was possible
was done to tempt them to take the last decisive step; and
when at last they arrived at Constantinople, they received the most cordial welcome and almost immediately
began to exercise great influence. For the next quarter

of a century, the family played an important role in the affairs of the state. Repeated episodes showed how far they were favored at the Sublime Porte and how they could count even on diplomatic support, when it seemed desirable, to serve their own vital interests or those of their coreligionists.

In order to appreciate the background of all this, it is necessary to rid one's mind of the nineteenth-century antithesis between the civilized West and the backward East, the amenities of the occidental world and the discomforts of the Levant, the humane environment of the Christendom and Moslem semi-barbarism. That, so far as it was ever true, belonged to the future. In the sixteenth century, Turkey was superior to the Occident in military power, equal in architecture and public works, hardly second as regards the amenities of life. What was more important, she was certainly not inferior in humanity. If the wars waged by the Grand Turk were cruel and barbaric, those waged by the Christian powers were no less so. When Charles V captured Tunis in 1535, thousands of men and women were killed or enslaved in an orgy of bloodshed. Nor was this the case only when infidels were in question: the sack of Rome in 1527 by the emperor's forces was hardly less appalling than the sack of Constantinople by the Turks in 1453. The forays of the Knights of Malta and other Christian paladins, in the name of religion, were as pitiless and indiscriminate as those of the Corsairs (often in fact recent converts) who sailed under the Crescent. Nothing in Moslem annals of the time was as bloodthirsty as the Massacre of St. Bartholomew in France. Though the Turks did not always respect diplomatic immunities, they never per-

petrated in this sphere any worse crime than the king of
Hungary's barbarous butchery of the sultan's ambassador before the Battle of Mohacs in 1526, or for that
matter that of the French envoys by the Spaniards in 1541
in Milan. The palace tragedies of Suleiman the Magnificent were no more gruesome than those at the court of
his contemporary, King Henry VIII of England. The
exaction of a tithe of their male children from the defeated
Christians, to fill the ranks of the janissaries, was out-
done in cruelty by the kidnapping of Jewish children in
Portugal a generation before to bring them up as Christians. Recruiting the imperial harem from captured
Christian beauties was humanity itself if contrasted with
the systematic dishonoring and then murder of beautiful
Moslem captives by some of the Christian sea-captains
of the time. No man was persecuted for his religion
in sixteenth-century Turkey, when all over Europe —
not only in Spain — Inquisitions were at work and the
skies were reddened by the glare of the pyres in which
thousands of unbelievers perished. In matters of personal
hygiene, there was no question where the superiority
lay: cleanliness in Constantinople was reckoned an
integral part of godliness, and the Turks jeered unmerci-
fully at their western European contemporaries who did
not wash their bodies all over more than twice between
birth and death. In transferring himself from West to
East, a man hardly descended in the scale of material
amenities, not at all in that of essential civilization.

These were the conditions, then, which Doña Gracia
found when she arrived in Turkey at the beginning of
1553. She and her family took up their abode, not in
Constantinople proper where most of the Jews then lived,

but with the rest of the European colony in the fashionable suburb of Galata, or Pera, beyond the Golden Horn.
In a later generation, the distribution of population was
to change and this area was to receive a predominantly
Jewish character; but at that time the traders and pedlars
who swarmed over the narrow strip of water to open their
stalls by day returned home to their own quarter by
night. Here Doña Gracia had a lovely house, surrounded
by a garden, the rent of which was said to be no less than
a ducat each day. (It may be that this was the same
mansion, in the suburb of Ortakewy, which was subsequently known as the Palace of Belvedere, where her
nephew resided in such state later on.)

She lived in princely style, in an environment which
was in Turkey but not of it. The charity that she dispensed was tremendous. Eighty paupers were fed each
day at her table. ("Something must be wrong; must have
cheated people somewhere," spitefully reported Hans
Dernschwam, unable to deny the meritorious act.) She
was waited on by an elaborate train of attendants, many
of whom had come with her from Flanders, or even from
Portugal, those who were New Christians like herself
adopting Judaism on their arrival if they had not done
so already.

Although in such close relations with the Sublime Porte
and constant intercourse with high officers of state, the
family nevertheless lived in a world of their own. It was
no oriental household, but reproduced on the banks of
the Bosphorus the domestic manners of a patrician family
of Lisbon, Antwerp, or Venice. With the assent (according to Andrés Laguna) of the sultan himself, the serving
women and attendants did not wear the old-world Spanish

wimples, like other Jewesses, but bodices and coifs in the
Venetian style. They preserved not only European dress
but an occidental manner of life. They used *Don* and
Señora as titles of respect. Their domestic habits were
Spanish. They spoke Spanish or Portuguese among
themselves. They carried on their correspondence in
Spanish; they heard sermons in the synagogue in the
same language; they read Spanish books; they had intercourse with Spanish savants. Their cuisine was more
reminiscent of Lisbon or Madrid than of the Golden
Horn. They conducted their households in the Spanish
or Italian styles; and they were kept in constant touch
with life in the Peninsula by the unending stream of
refugees from the fires of the Inquisition who came to
Turkey, in many cases under their auspices, in order to
seek shelter (in the beautiful Hebrew phrase) "under
the pinions of the Divine Presence." They were surrounded by a large circle of scholars, dependents, visitors,
servitors, mendicants, with a background much like their
own.

The average Jewish woman of Constantinople at this
time was, to be sure, hardly of this type. A description
written at the beginning of the seventeenth century
probably applies faithfully enough to the period of a
generation earlier. It is vivid, but hardly flattering in
some particulars:—[9]

The elder mabble their heads in linen, with the knots hanging
down behind. Others do wear high caps of plate, whereof some
I have seen of beaten gold. They wear long quilted waistcoats,
with breeches underneath, in winter of cloth, in summer of
linen; and over all, when they stir abroad, loose gowns of
purple flowing from the shoulders. They are generally fat and
rank of the savours which attend upon sluttish corpulency.

For the most part they are goggle-eyed. They neither shun conversation nor are too watchfully guarded by their husbands. They are good work-women, and can and will do anything for a profit, that is to be done by the art of a woman and which suits with the fashion of these countries. Upon injuries received or violence done to any of their nation, they will cry out mainly at their windows, beating their cheeks and tearing of their garments.... They are so skilled in lamentations, that the Greeks do hire them to cry at their funerals.

Doña Gracia's way was made easier for her to some extent by reason of the fact that it was no new thing for the Turks to see Jewish women even of this type busying themselves with public affairs and sometimes influencing them. An English contemporary presents a graphic picture of the background of their activity:[10] —

The sultanas have leave of the king that certain Jewes women may at any time come into the seraglio unto them, who being extraordinary subtle queans and coming in under the colour of teaching them some fine needlework, or showing them secrets in making waters, oils and painting-stuffs for their faces (having once made friendship with the eunuchs which keep the doors, by often bribing them) do make themselves by their crafty insinuation, so familiar with the king's women, that they rule them as they please, and do carry out anything to sell for them, and buy and bring in whatsoever the Sultanas shall have a will to. And hence it is, that all such Jewes women as frequent the seraglio do become very rich. For whatsoever they bring in they buy it cheap and sell it dear to them; and then on the contrary, when they have jewels to sell for the Sultanas (which are to be conveyed out by stealth) they receive their true value for them of strangers, and then tell the simple ladies, who know not the worth of them (and are afraid to be discovered) that they sold them peradventure for half that which they had for them. By these means there come things of great price out of the seraglio, to be sold at very easy rates; yet in the end the Jewes have but a bad market of it....

Foremost among these Court Jewesses, and probably one of the most busy persons in Constantinople at the time of Doña Gracia's arrival, was one named Esther,

now at the height of a reputation which was to continue
unabated for over half a century, and then to end with
gruesome tragicalness.[11] Her husband, Rabbi Elijah
Handali, had died after a very few years of marriage, so
that she was left to make her own way in the world. She
obtained an entrée into the imperial palaces and made
herself useful to the ladies of the harem in the Old Serai
(now reserved for women), who could not get along in their
silken captivity without some sort of outside contact.
She assisted them in childbirth, purchased them cosmetics,
brought them trinkets, told them news, carried their
messages, and in the end became utterly indispensable.
Suleiman the Magnificent himself recognized her services
generously and, as early as 1539, when she can barely
have been in her twenties, issued an imperial firman
according her and her descendants special privileges and
exemption from taxation. Generally, she was now known
as Esther Kyra, this being the title universally given in
Turkey to these Court Jewesses, of whom, as we have
seen, there were several at this time.[12]

In domestic affairs she sometimes exercised a boundless influence, in more reigns than one. It was to the
women of the harem that the sultan so often listened
when any appointment was to be made; and the latter
listened to Esther Kyra, who, after the fashion of the
time, received gifts from those whom she nominated.
Her reputation and power thus grew apace. In the words
of the Hebrew chronicler, "All the officials bowed down
and prostrated themselves before her, and all those who
desired aught from the sultan came and went forth at her
bidding." She took the opportunity to secure various
trading concessions; and what with these and the routine

gifts she received, she became extremely wealthy. In her prosperity she did not forget her fellow Jews. She was immensely charitable, fed the poor at her own table, came to their assistance after the great fire of 1569 which reduced the Jewish quarter of Constantinople to rubble, supported scholars such as the antiquarian Samuel Sullam and the lame Isaac Akrish, and defrayed the expenses of the publication of Hebrew books. On the other hand, she demanded deferential treatment; and a case is on record when she intervened while a complicated question of divorce was being discussed before the rabbinical tribunal and extracted a decision in accordance with her personal desires. It may be that it was she who first introduced Doña Gracia to Court circles on her arrival in Constantinople.

Doubtless the latter could also rely on the assistance of those other Jewesses who had an entrée to the imperial palace. Typical of them was Esperanza Malchi, the sultana's tirewoman, a letter of whose to Queen Elizabeth of England has been preserved: [13]—

To the most Serene Queen of England, France and Ireland:
As the sun with his rays shines upon the Earth, so the virtue and greatness of your Majesty extend over the whole Universe, so much so that those who are of different nations and laws desire to serve your Majesty. This I say as to myself, who, being a Hebrew by law and nation, have, from the first hour that it pleased the Lord God to put into the hearts of this our most serene Queen Mother to make use of my services, ever been desirous that an occasion might arise on which I might show that disposition which I cherish. Besides your Majesty having sent a distinguished Ambassador into this Kingdom, with a present for this most serene Queen, my mistress, in as much as she has been willing to make use of my services, she has found me ready. And now at the departure of the noble Ambassador alluded to, the most serene Queen, wishing to prove to your Majesty the love she bears you, sends to your

Majesty by the same illustrious Ambassador a robe and a girdle, and two kerchiefs wrought in gold, and three wrought in silk, after the fashion of this Kingdom, and a necklace of pearls and rubies; the whole the most serene Queen sends to the illustrious Ambassador by the hand of the Sieur Bostanggi Basi; and by my own hand I have delivered to the illustrious Ambassador a wreath of diamonds from the jewels of her Highness, which, she says, your Majesty will be pleased to wear for the love of her, and give information of the receipt. And your Majesty being a lady full of condescension, I venture to proffer the following request; namely, that, since there are to be met with in your Kingdom distilled waters of every description for the face and odiferous oils for the hands, your Majesty would favor me by transmitting some by my hand for this most serene Queen by my hand, as, being articles for ladies, she does not wish them to pass through other hands. Likewise, if there are to be had in your Kingdom cloths of silk or wool, articles of fancy suited for so high a Queen as my Mistress, your Majesty may be pleased to send them, as she will be more gratified by such objects than any valuable your Majesty could send her. I have nothing further to add, but to pray the Lord God that he may give your Majesty the victory over your enemies; and that your Majesty may ever be prosperous and happy. Amen.

Your Majesty's most humble
Esperanza Malchi

With the domicile of the Nasi family in Turkey and the arrival to maturity of the younger Gracia (now married to her cousin, Samuel Nasi), the time came for a final settlement of the long-standing dispute about the family property, which apparently now blazed up again. Ever since her brother-in-law's death in Antwerp, some ten or twelve years before, Doña Gracia had administered this alone, in accordance with the terms of his will. Her sister and niece now reasserted their claim on one-half of it, in addition presumably to his very considerable personal estate. Doña Gracia, on the other hand, maintained that the capital of the firm had originally belonged to her husband, Francisco Mendes, founder of the family and of the family fortune, and thus devolved by inheritance upon her and her daughter. To this the other side replied that, on his death, Francisco had left half of his estate to his brother Diogo, in recognition of the share he had taken in building up the business he controlled, and it was this half that they claimed. Gracia retorted that her husband had lived and died as a nominal Christian in Portugal, and Portuguese law had therefore to be followed in dividing his estate. According to this, however, half of a man's property legally devolved, upon his death, on his widow, and two-thirds of what was left on the orphans, leaving only an insignificant fraction of one-sixth which might be disposed of arbitrarily by will: and this arrangement had been confirmed in the formal contract between her and her husband drawn up by a notary public at the time of their marriage. Hence he did not have the right to dispose of his estate in the way the others said that he had done, and their claim was only fractional. Moreover, she had incurred very great expense in order to save the family property during the critical periods when it was menaced with confiscation, both in Antwerp and in Venice — the last, a direct result of her sister's foolhardiness: surely, she was not legally obliged to bear the financial responsibility alone or, in the latter case, at all; and the same applied also to what she had been compelled to spend in France for the same reason. All this had completely consumed the one-sixth of her husband's estate which was all that had (according to her) legally devolved on Diogo: and she had accordingly no further obligation to his widow and daughter — who were, however, wealthy enough, as it seems, without this.

The matter had to be decided by the rabbis, for the Jews of Turkey enjoyed legal autonomy. But a most awkward technical problem presented itself. If the dispute were to be adjudicated in accordance with talmudic law, then there was reason to act in accordance with the terms of Francisco's testament, and Doña Gracia would have been compelled to surrender to her sister a good portion of her fortune. If, on the other hand, Marrano families before they left the Peninsula were to be considered as being bound up to that time by the personal law of their country of residence, that document had no validity and her estate would be left intact. The rabbis were therefore placed in the interesting position of having to argue whether in such cases as this the talmudic law which they administered with such fervor was to be applied retrospectively.

The whole question, formulated in elegant Hebrew (obviously by an expert hand) and containing a wealth of incidental information which is invaluable for the reconstruction of Doña Gracia's biography and the family history at large, was argued at great length in 1554-5, with a host of subsidiary details, before some of the most eminent oriental Talmudists of the time — Joseph ibn Leb, Joshua Soncino, Samuel de Medina, Moses di Trani and Joseph Caro. (In the published responsa of these scholars all the documents are to be found, with the names transparently disguised, in a fashion that leaves no room for doubt as to the eminent personalities actually concerned.) Though the approaches to the problem differed, the decisions of all except, in certain respects, the last-named favored Doña Gracia's claim; for it was obvious that, if a verdict were given in favor of her sister, it would

imply that all contracts between Marranos which had
been made according to local law were invalid, and
inextricable confusion would result; one of the scholars
consulted felt, however, impelled to note that he had
"shown no grace to Gracia" in considering the question.[14]
Thus, therefore, the matter was left. Henceforth, the
capital at her command was unquestionably hers.

The reason for the intense concern manifested by the
Turkish statesmen in Doña Gracia's transference to Constantinople was not, of course, by any means altruistic.
They were interested not in the family but in the family
fortune, one of the greatest in Europe, and in the commercial activity that might follow in its wake. It was
hardly possible in those days (as it is in these) to enjoy
an income from capital by the process of investment, except in land — and in the circumstances of the family history that was out of the question in their case. If she was
not to live on her fortune and progressively exhaust it,
Doña Gracia had to use it therefore in trade. Moreover,
she had invested a good part of it in merchandise, which
continued to arrive long after she had settled in Constantinople, and which had to be disposed of there. The
sultan looked on approvingly. The Turks were themselves a relatively small caste of warrior-farmers, without
urban tastes and lacking both inclination and ability for
commerce. This they were content to leave to the non-
Moslems. But the Christians were of questionable
fidelity. Only the Jews were bound to the Ottoman
empire by ties, not only of gratitude, but also of inevi-
tability; and it was thus obviously to the advantage of
the state that trade should be in their hands rather than

that of the Greeks or Armenians or Italians. Thus the transference of the former business interests of the House of Mendes to the shores of the Bosphorus was supremely gratifying to the Turkish authorities. In Antwerp the firm, though important, had been one of many; here, it was for a time very nearly supreme.

According to the agent of the Fuggers, Hans Dernschwam, who has been cited before, Doña Gracia carried on a large overseas business in wool, pepper and grain with Venice and Italy. Most important probably were the imports of cloth and textiles, which were distributed throughout the empire, Turkish raw products being exported in return. The operations were on such a scale that Doña Gracia had her own ships to carry the goods; and it was said that she even built them.

The ramifications of the firm were wide. There were agents and agencies all over the Balkans and the Archipelago (certainly in Ragusa, Belgrade, Sarajevo and Naxos) and in Italy (e. g., Ancona, Ferrara and Venice) as well as at Lyons and elsewhere. Former Marranos were in its employment in every part of Europe. The Turkish government found it worth while to give these mercantile activities special protection. In the unruly circumstances of the time this was something supremely necessary. Thus, in 1565, six men in Doña Gracia's service, who had embarked on a river-vessel for Vidin, on the right bank of the Danube (in what is now Bulgaria), disappeared during the course of the voyage; at about the same time, a ship in charge of four of her agents was pillaged in the port of Santorin in the Archipelago, the stolen merchandise being sold in Naxos and the local authorities enforcing in her favor only partial indemnifi-

cation. Her influence in Court circles was such that she
was able to secure imperial firmans ordering justice to
be done in the one case and proper compensation exacted
in the other.[15]

So great was the volume of her merchandise that passed
through Ragusa that she was able to conclude a special
arrangement concerning it with the government of that
republic. In the letter of application submitted on her
behalf by her agents, in a somewhat awkward Italian,
shortly after her arrival in Turkey, she tactfully recalled
the cordial welcome she had received when she passed
through the city in the previous year, and then explained
how she now proposed to trade with Italy and other
lands. Owing to her absence (or it might have been
better termed, her flight) from that country, she feared
that certain difficulties might arise, and an attempt even
made (presumably on the pretext of her apostasy) to place
an embargo on her property while it was en route. She
therefore asked for a safe-conduct for her goods, as well
as for her representatives, on their way through the city;
otherwise she would (she indicated) be compelled to find
another transit port. If any legitimate claim were made
on her, she pointed out with some pride, she was in a
position to meet it, however great the sum involved.
Her petition was granted in the council by 30 votes to 7,
though seven of those who supported the majority did
not think that the concession should last for as long as
five years, which was approved by only 23 votes to 14.

Well before this, indeed, her consignments, mainly of
textiles, had begun to appear in the Ragusa customs
house in accordance with the terms of the original agreement made at the time of her flight from Italy; and we

learn how in June, 1555, a parcel of linen from Venice was allowed to be forwarded to Turkey notwithstanding some slight obstacle that had arisen. The original agreement of 1552 was renewed on its expiration in 1557 for another five years, after discussion by the council of the republic at its session of August 7, and again on July 4, 1562. At this time she inquired whether she might make a special arrangement in connection with the payment of the customs duties and was given leave to deposit a pledge for unpaid amounts in the same manner as was allowed to citizens of the republic. She had, indeed, no guarantor of sufficient calibre in the city; but in view of the special circumstances a declaration in her own name or that of her nephew, Joseph Nasi (João Miguez) was accepted. On her side, she undertook to continue to make use of the port, and to persuade other Jewish merchants to do likewise. She negotiated with the petty republic, in short, almost like an independent power.

Such was the consideration with which she was regarded that part of it descended on her local agents, Abner Alfarin and Isaac Ergas. They were treated in the city with the utmost deference, being permitted even to live outside the quarter to which the other Jews had been confined in 1545. When, in 1558, there was a dispute regarding the payment of the ghetto tax, they assumed responsibility for the area as a whole at a minimum rate of 60 scudi annually, on the understanding that their own residences would be excluded from the arrangements.

On several occasions, the authorities at Ragusa made use of Doña Gracia's services for the purpose of sending remittances abroad. Thus in July, 1557, because of the danger of direct transmission, she was requested to pay

THE FORMER GHETTO AT RAGUSA (DUBROVNIK)
entrance to the synagogue is on the left

Fille Iuisue d'Andrinople.

A Turkish Jewish Maiden

a sum of no less than 3,100 ducats for some special purpose to two envoys of the republic then in Constantinople.
Two years later, her services were again utilized for the
transmission of a credit of 1,000 ducats, and again for 400
ducats in the following year. Such transactions and
manipulations could, of course, be turned to good service
when the circumstances demanded; on the first occasion,
for example, her Ragusa agents suggested that advantage
should be taken of this special opportunity to make certain payments in her name at Venice through the medium
of the Ragusan government — a process normally very
difficult for her, owing to her earlier experiences.[16] Only
the arrangements which Doña Gracia concluded at
Ragusa have been preserved; it is probable that similar
agreements were made with other trading cities, no less
eager for her patronage. It is abundantly clear that the
House was considered in Mediterranean commerce a force
to be conciliated, cajoled and attracted.

In Italy her principal representative was her husband's
kinsman, Agostino Enriques, still living in Ferrara. He
had long been associated with her affairs and, as has been
mentioned, been designated by Diogo Mendes in his will
as joint-guardian for his daughter should it be necessary.
When she left for Turkey, she made over all her Italian
property into his charge, arranging for the income to be
paid over to him on condition that he accounted for it
punctually to her. Her French capital, on the other hand,
was held in the name of Luca degli Albizzi and another
Florentine: but the accumulated interest on this also, to
the total amount of 18,000 ducats, was entrusted to
Enriques to be used as capital for his business ventures
in partnership with the poet-businessman Duarte Gomez,

each of whom was to add 3,000 ducats of his own to the sum.[17] This venture proved outstandingly successful. It was said that the two had correspondents in Flanders, Spain, Constantinople and France. In Venice they were prominent on the Rialto. They sent their galleys to sea on commercial ventures; and, since as foreigners they were unable to do this legally, they enlisted the services of a local youth in whose name they traded and who obtained for them through his father, a Venetian patrician, whatever privileges they needed. Because of their great wealth and with their Spanish wiles, it was said, they enjoyed great advantages on the occasion of their visits to Venice and were able to do anything they wanted, going in and out of the houses of the nobility with their wives on equal terms. Enriques was alleged to have doubled his original capital of 50,000 ducats by his diabolical arts — the principal one of which, no doubt, was thrift. The total amount of Doña Gracia's investments in Italy was calculated at some 35,000 ducats. When we recall that the sums here in question were only incidentals of the enormous family fortune, it becomes apparent how immensely wealthy she was.

Early in 1554 she was joined in Constantinople by her nephew, João Miguez, who after settling his affairs elsewhere now followed the example of the rest of the family. That April, shortly after his arrival, he formally adopted Judaism, and in the following August was married with great pomp to his cousin Reyna, Gracia's daughter, with whom his name had been coupled for so long, ever since the flight from Antwerp. Henceforth, as a Jew, he went by the name of Joseph Nasi. His career reads like a fantastic story out of the Arabian nights — how he began to enter political life, how he attached himself to the party of the Crown Prince, Selim, how on the latter's accession to the throne he became a power in the land, how he was courted by all the statesmen of Europe, how he used diplomatic action to settle up his old scores with foreign governments, how, in 1566, he was actually created Duke of Naxos and the Cyclades. The details of this amazing story must be left for the moment.[18] It is obvious, however, that his growing influence at Court afforded Doña Gracia an ever readier entrée and gave her greater opportunities for action, when she found it necessary. Above all, his intimacy (not, it was rumored, disinterested) with Sultan Suleiman's avaricious son-in-law, Rustam Pasha, who was grand vizier with only a short break from 1544 to 1561, proved particularly valuable to her; for as a result of this the family henceforth had much direct political influence and received support consistently at the Sublime Porte.

From the moment of his arrival in Turkey, Joseph Nasi (as he must now be called) was closely connected with his aunt in all her enterprises, whether economic or beneficent. He was associated with her in trade, represented her whether in private or public whenever it was necessary and generally figured as her spokesman. On the other hand, so long as she lived he acted only a subordinate role. He may have cut a greater figure in the public eye, granted interviews in her name, enjoyed public dignities, played the noble. But when there was any good to be done or any positive action to be taken, it was Doña Gracia who provided the backing, the inspiration and the driving force which he sometimes lacked.

Other old friends had also come to join the circle in
Turkey. In 1558, owing to the action of the Grand
Inquisitor of the Roman Holy Office, Cardinal Ghislieri,
the Marrano literary circle at Ferrara had been broken
up.[19] Its best-known members made their way eastwards.
Of Abraham Usque, the printer, there is no further trace.
His son Salomon removed at first to Venice (where in the
following year a Purim play written by him was presented
before an audience which included a number of the
nobility and gentry). Later on he settled in Constantinople, bringing with him the types used in his father's
press and at least one of the assistants. For a short
while he maintained a Hebrew printing house, not, however, very productive. At the same time, he engaged in
trade — perhaps òn account of the House of Nasi, which
must have given employment to a relatively considerable
proportion of the Jews of the capital at this time. In
connection with this he went backwards and forwards
between Turkey and Italy, which he visited more than
once; and while in Venice, in 1567, he published his
Spanish translation of Petrarch's sonnets, still very highly
esteemed, which he dedicated to Alessandro Farnese,
Prince of Parma. (Duarte Gomez, who had himself
translated Petrarch into the same language, contributed
an introductory sonnet.) His knowledge of languages
and his experience of many countries brought him into
touch with the foreign diplomatic colony in Constantinople, including the English representative, who presumably found him useful both as adviser and as interpreter.
Years later, in his old age, when Sultan Murad III died,
he wrote a report on conditions at the Turkish Court
(accompanied by a couple of sonnets in florid Italian)

which the ambassador hastened to send to England, where they were studied and annotated by Lord Burleigh, Queen Elizabeth's secretary of state.[20]

The most interesting member of the Usque family, who had been in closest touch with Doña Gracia, was Samuel Usque, who had composed his great historic prose-poem, *Consolation for the Tribulations of Israel*, while she was resident in Ferrara, and not only dedicated it to her but immortalized her qualities in the text. He, it seems, now settled in Safed, where his credulity in spreading sensational stories about the discovery of the Lost Ten Tribes and his advanced apocalyptic views got him into some trouble even in that city of mystics and cabalists. He has been identified on over-slender evidence with the "Samuel" who was in the employment of Doña Gracia and once went on a mission to Naxos on her behalf.[21] But it may be conjectured that he was a better stylist than businessman, and that his eminent patroness was abundantly aware of the fact.

The year after her arrival in the Turkish capital, Doña Gracia executed a pious commission which had been entrusted to her by her husband on his death, nearly twenty years before. The Marranos had preserved, like other Jews, a nostalgic longing for the Holy Land, heightened perhaps by the tragedy of their own lives. (This continued down to our own day, when the remnant of these crypto-Jewish communities, discovered in northern Portugal, were found to have added the phrase, "as our brethren do in the Land of Promise," to the stereotyped formula of benediction on the performance of a religious duty, which they had preserved from the traditional ritual.) Francisco Mendes, therefore, had desired to be buried in Palestine where, according to the traditional interpretation of the last song of Moses, "the Land atoneth for the People" (Deuteronomy 32.43), whatever their sin (and what sin could be greater than to dissemble one's faith?) even after death. Gracia had promised to perform this pious service for him when it should become possible. The time for fulfilling her promise had now arrived. Somehow — it must have been a hazardous task — she managed to get her husband's remains exhumed from the churchyard where they had been buried in Lisbon, and taken to be laid again to rest finally outside Jerusalem, in the Valley of Jehoshaphat, the traditional burial-place of pious Jews for a hundred generations; ample largesse being bestowed at this time on the poor.[22]

This was the earliest manifestation of the intense Palestinophile tendencies of the Nasi family, which were later to become so marked as to cause them to be numbered among the great pioneers of the modern Zionist movement. With that great consummation, however, the Duke of Naxos was principally concerned, as will be seen at a later stage.[23]

Meanwhile, in ecclesiastical circles in Italy, the episode of her flight had not been forgotten, though the names of the two sisters were confused. In a report on the New Christians of Portugal and their vicissitudes in Italy, drawn up by a zealous son of the Church in 1564, her career was cited as the crowning instance of their disgraceful way of life:—[24]

Nor is there any city in Italy where there are not to be found Portuguese Marranos who have fled from the Inquisition in Portugal. These become wealthy, because they trade in all manner of commodities without restriction, just like Christians. They then transfer themselves to Turkey, where they inform the Grand Turk of all that is done here. Among these there is a very wealthy Portuguese woman, named Madonna Brianda, who lived for a long time at Ferrara and Venice as a Christian. Then she went to Turkey and married her daughter with a son of the Grand Turk's physician, and now lives in the Law of Moses, she and all her family.

There was indeed good reason for this scandalized remembrance. For the Nasi family had borne away with them, not only a great part of their wealth, but also a spirit of natural human resentment, which in due course was to show its fruit.

CHAPTER VI

"The Heart of Her People"

FROM her splendid residence in Galata, overlooking the Bosphorus, Doña Gracia all but dominated Jewish life in the Turkish Empire and beyond for a dozen years — the only woman who ever played such a role in the history of the Diaspora. The Jewish fortitude that had saved so many Marranos from the burning Inquisitional furnace now knew no impediment, while the force of character that had once intimidated even the queen regent of the Netherlands was in no wise diminished with the approach of age. Hans Dernschwam, the shrewd German business-man, expressed his recognition of her outstanding ability in a decided though to us cryptic fashion: "She is a dangerous woman, like Barbara of Cologne."[1] So long as Gracia lived, her nephew, Joseph Nasi, the subsequent Duke of Naxos, seems to have played in reality a second-ary role, whatever the world might think. It was she who had the initiative in everything; he followed obediently in her trail. Her coreligionists throughout Turkey spoke of her in her day by no other title than *La Señora* or, in Hebrew, *ha-Geveret* — "the Lady," with no further qual-ification.[2]

Memorable above all was the great work of rescue which she continued uninterruptedly, in her new home as in the old, on behalf of the still-harried Marranos of Spain and Portugal. As before, we know no precise

122

details. On the other hand, after her death, Saadiah Lungo, *hazzan* or Reader at one of the Salonica synagogues and perhaps the most prolific and melodious of the Hebrew poets of the time, singled out this aspect of her activity for special mention in his commemorative elegy. In obscure phrases, in accordance with the unfortunate poetical convention of that age, he gave an account of the persecutions in Portugal, stating that in this tragic generation the Jewish people would have been entirely lost had not God raised up for them "a remnant of the House of Nasi" who made smooth the path of fugitives who wished to return to their God. She stood, he continued, at the roadside, in the Tent of Abraham:—[3]

... to receive the groaning wayfarers who return to the service of their Creator so tired and weary that every knee would have faltered but for this great House, which was appointed from Heaven to have mercy upon them. . . . Every soul of the House of Jacob that comes to take refuge under the Pinions of the Divine Presence — she was their mother and suckled them from her comforting breast.

They are memorable words and clearly denote the continuation after her arrival in Turkey of the work of relief in which she had been immersed while living at Ferrara. Similarly, Joshua Soncino, one of the few contemporary rabbis who dared to oppose her, refers,[4] though in a similarly cryptic style, to the manner in which she

assisted the poor and helpless, to deliver them and give them rest, in this world and the next,

and how

she acquired merit and bestowed it upon others, delivering their soul from darkness and bringing forth from the murk of the vanities of the world those who lived in gloom and obscurity, prisoners of the deathly guile of men who say "Strip ye! Strip ye! Let not the name of Israel be mentioned more."

The allusion seems obvious, though once again, unfortunately, we are given no details.[5]

That she was charitable goes without saying — this was the hall-mark of her people, "merciful sons of merciful sires." But her charity was literally boundless, extending over many lands and knowing no limit as to object. Eighty mendicants, we are told, sat down each day at her table, and blessed her name. No Jewess could be deaf to the call of her coreligionists in Palestine: and here too (as we have seen) her benefactions were known and her fame universal. At every moment of trouble and distress in the community, she was certainly foremost in the work of relief. If news arrived of the enslavement of unoffending Jews by the Knights of Malta, when they captured Turkish merchant-vessels at sea or made forays on the infidel coast, she would have been the first person to open her purse in order to collaborate in the great *mitzvah* of the Redemption of the Slaves. At the time of the periodical outbreaks of pestilence in the Turkish empire, in 1554, 1556 and 1561 — when Don Salomon Senior in Salonica put his entire fortune at the disposal of charity, and Moses Jachia and his son Gedaliah expended thousands of ducats to aid the sufferers — it is certain that she would not have allowed herself to be left behind; and in the last year of her life, she cannot have been backward during the terrible winter of 1567/8, which caused untold misery to the poorer Turkish Jews. She lavishly supported hospitals, synagogues, schools and scholars all over the Ottoman empire.

The central institution which owed its existence to her was an academy or *yeshiva*, which she established in the crowded Balata district in Constantinople. Here, pious householders began to come together every day for worship as well as for study, so that in due course there came into existence by the side of the academy a new place of worship, also lavishly endowed, which long continued to be known after the foundress as "the Synagogue of the *Señora*." This development led to some serious complications, for in order to prevent disputes it was generally customary in Jewish communities of the past for members to be forbidden to attach themselves to, or even to attend service in, any synagogue other than the one to which they originally belonged. Doña Gracia, however, considered that this regulation need not apply in the present case, where there was no element of competition or rivalry; and in order to gratify her the Constantinople communities, when they settled the details of communal taxation, formally decided to suspend it. Moreover, at various communal conferences, at the request of the House of Nasi, it was formally decided that there should henceforth be no restriction on the right of the members of any community in Constantinople to go for worship where they pleased. Hence the new congregation increased and flourished. It was recruited especially, at the specific invitation of the foundress, by various members of the Synagogue of the Spanish Exiles[6] — presumably the first of those which had been set up by the refugees from Spain in 1492 — which was in the immediate neighborhood. So far did the drift proceed that the directors of the latter community became seriously alarmed and passed a new regulation forbidding its members to attend any synagogue other than their own, under pain of excommunication. The dispute now grew to such an extent that an appeal was made to certain leading

rabbis[7] for a definite ruling in the matter. They decided
that, in the circumstances which prevailed in the capital,
a great city with many communities, where no such
restriction was now generally recognized, a *Hascama* of
this sort was impracticable, illogical and therefore invalid:
for in fact it depended merely on the assent and good
will of those who chose to adhere to it.

The Synagogue of the *Señora* thus continued to flourish,
not only during the lifetime of the foundress, but long
after. Destroyed in the great fire of 1660, which reduced
Istanbul to ashes and was particularly disastrous to the
Jews, it was subsequently rebuilt and continued in existence (latterly in the Haskeuy district) down almost to
our own day.

The synagogue was at the outset subsidiary to the
great *yeshiva* or academy which was annexed to it, as to
every other place of worship in the capital at this time.
Generously financed and warmly supported, this had for
a long time a deservedly great reputation. Its first principal was the famous Joseph ibn Leb, who had been born
about the beginning of the sixteenth century at Monastir
(probably of Spanish parentage) and afterwards lived in
Brusa and then in Salonica. When he was compelled to
flee from this city, owing to the devastating outbreak of
plague in 1545, he made his way to Constantinople,
brokenhearted at the recent death of one of his two sons
at the hands of an assassin (perhaps one of the father's
personal enemies), and the other by drowning. There, in
due course, he was appointed by Doña Gracia to preside
over her new academy, the "Academy of the [Spanish]
Exiles, that is in the House of the *Geveret*, Gracia Nasi,"
as it was officially called. He remained *Rosh Yeshiva*, or

Director, of this institution for many years, until failing health made it impossible for him to continue his work. He was regarded as one of the most eminent Turkish rabbis and Talmudists of his age, one of his projects being the publication of a popular code of Jewish law similar to the *Shulhan Arukh* of Joseph Caro. In this, he was forestalled by his great contemporary. Nevertheless, four volumes of closely-argued responsa remain as a memorial of his acumen (the second was prepared for the press, he informs us, in Constantinople when he was "in the company of the devoted students, votaries of knowledge . . . in the *Yeshiva* of the Crowned Lady, crown of good family and piety, the Lady Gracia Nasi"). But he was, too, a man of character and, notwithstanding an unhappy episode earlier in his career, when he was physically assaulted in the streets of Salonica by a wealthy ex-Marrano whom he had offended, he retained his independence of mind even where his patrons were intimately concerned. (He had been comforted perhaps by the consideration that a fire broke out on the very same night in the shop in front of which the episode had occurred, and destroyed half the city!) In the heat of argument some of his opponents occasionally hinted that he was over-obsequious, but this could not be maintained seriously. His successor was one Yom-tob Cohen, "Principal of the Academy of the *Geveret*," of whom we know little save that he died in Adrianople, broken by the news of his son's murder, and was commemorated in an elegy by Saadiah Lungo. Later on, in the seventeenth century, the same position was held by Rabbi Moses ben Nissim Benveniste, perhaps a remote relative of the foundress, a renowned linguist.[8]

Doña Gracia's munificence extended as we have seen beyond the capital. It was natural that her interest was greatest in those places where her fellow-Marranos had settled. At this time, Salonica was their great city of refuge: it was said that no fewer than 10,000 arrived there within these few years. They attached themselves at the outset to the "Lisbon" synagogue — one of the score or more of regional communities which then flourished in the city.[9] After the Inquisition began its activity in Portugal, the increase in number made this body almost unmanageable. In 1536, the newcomers from Evora broke off and created their own synagogue, which was richly endowed by the wealthy Joseph Pinto. Some fourteen years later, there was another secession, the original congregation being subdivided henceforth into the New and Old Lisbon Synagogues. But still, the Marrano influx continued without remission. In order to avoid further friction, for it seems that the existing communities competed among themselves for the wealthy and cultured newcomers, Doña Gracia came to the conclusion that it was desirable for a separate organization to be established for them. Accordingly, at the close of 1559, she set up a fresh synagogue on their behalf, her nephew, Don Joseph Nasi, acting as her representative in the preliminary negotiations. It was currently known, it seems, as the Wayfarers' Synagogue (*Kahal Orahim*), but officially it had the beautiful title *Livyat Hen*, or "The Chaplet of Grace," in delicate allusion to the foundress' own name. Later, it came to be called the Jachia Synagogue, after a local maecenas, Don Solomon ibn Jachia, in whose *cortijo*, or courtyard, the building was ultimately situated. It retained its individuality under this name until the great fire which devastated the city in 1917 and destroyed the historic physiognomy of its Jewish quarter.

Shortly after its foundation, the Lisbon Synagogue entered into a formal agreement with the new congregation, recognizing that all new immigrants from the Peninsula were to be attached to it henceforth. Notwithstanding the jealousy of the other Salonica communities, which resented the establishment of yet another place of worship, above all at a period when they were attempting to bring about a greater degree of centralization, the *Livyat Hen* flourished, attracting members also from some of the existing bodies. Of course, it continued to be lavishly supported by the foundress. The first rabbi, nominated by Don Joseph in December, 1559, was Moses Almosnino, one of the most erudite, eloquent and versatile of the local scholars, whose grandfather and great-grandfather had been martyred by the Inquisition. The conditions which he stipulated on accepting office were curious but highly characteristic of the man and of the time: first, that all the members should attend services on Mondays and Thursdays, when Scriptural readings were included in the ritual, as well as on Saturdays; secondly, that no quarrel between members should be allowed to continue for longer than two days without being submitted to arbitration; thirdly, that discipline should be practiced by the humbler members and generosity by the wealthier, who were to uphold the full communal burden in return for exercising full communal control. His inaugural sermon, filled with ecstatic eulogy of the pious foundress and her representative, has been preserved.[10] As we shall see, he long remained in intimate touch with the family.

Another pious foundation established by Doña Gracia in Salonica was a *Midrash*[11] for the study of rabbinic literature, for the upkeep of which she made over the rent of a number of houses which she owned in the city. This institution was organized according to a novel system. Normally, such academies maintained a number of scholars who studied in them perpetually, without any ulterior object. This one, on the other hand, had only one permanent member — its principal, Rabbi Samuel de Medina, one of the greatest Talmudists of the age. No other scholar was to be admitted to it for more than a limited period, during which he was to pursue his studies under the direction of the principal. Thus, all the rabbis of the city were able to enjoy the benefactress' bounty in rotation, instead of only a few fortunate individuals. Moreover, this arrangement, instead of encouraging cloistered students, in effect provided bursaries and "refresher courses" (as they would be termed today) for the local scholars who normally had to take their part in the general life of the community to the detriment of their studies.[12] It is not perhaps too much to suggest that this arrangement reflects Doña Gracia's relatively advanced views in the matter of what we would now call Higher Education.

Elsewhere, too, she earned a reputation as a patroness of Jewish learning. A contemporary rabbi speaks of her as "hewing the pillars of wisdom" by establishing houses of study for all who cared to attend. For example, when the Jewish settlement at Tiberias was revived under her auspices and those of her nephew,[13] she maintained and long supported a talmudical academy which, however, decayed soon after her death. Such feminine enthusiasm, it may be added, was not exceptional at this time, for though women did not participate in the activities of these bodies, they were profoundly interested in them. In the following generation, we are informed of another ex-Marrano woman, also named Gracia, daughter of the learned Immanuel Aboab, who on the death of her Christian husband (a Florentine noble) went to Palestine and for more than a quarter of a century administered the family benefactions there and directed the affairs of two rabbinical academies, one in Jerusalem and one in Safed. Such were the enthusiasms of Jewish women in that heroic age.

It is not very difficult to reconstruct a mental picture of the redoubtable but lovable matriarch. Clearly, she had the failings of her qualities. She knew to what family she belonged, and it does not seem that she was prepared to let others forget it. She was intensely generous, but considered that those who paid the piper had every right to call the tune. She was certainly impatient of opposition, at any sign of which her resentment flared up. But it seems that she was easily enough pacified in due course, and her anger seldom lasted long. It is noteworthy that one of those scholars who opposed her most fiercely at one stage, as will be seen later, spoke of her nevertheless in the most flattering terms, and that she did not mind submitting for his decision matters which deeply affected her personal interests. Although (or was it because?) she was brought up outside the pale of Judaism, she had, it seems, an exceptional veneration for rabbis and rabbinic scholarship, and it may be imagined that the readiest way to open the strings of her heart and her purse was through a display of piety and erudition. Her religiosity may have been seasoned with superstition — it would have been characteristic enough of the age and circumstances, as well as of her type. But the salient characteristic in her nature was, without doubt, her intense Jewish pride and her swift reactions to any report of injustice or persecution perpetrated against her coreligionists anywhere. On such occasions as this, no effort was too much and no expenditure too great; and the Nasi palace was kept in a perpetual turmoil, messengers being constantly dispatched and emissaries constantly received, until some measure of protection and retaliation had been set on foot.

All these good works resulted in the outpouring upon Doña Gracia Nasi during her lifetime of an unparalleled flood of admiration and of love on the part of her coreligionists. There was hardly any limit to the admiration with which she was spoken of and regarded by her contemporaries. Immanuel Aboab, the ex-Marrano chronicler of Hebrew literature, spoke of her "excellent virtues and noble deeds, regarding which it would be possible to write many books." Amatus Lusitanus, the physician, described her as being "adorned by all the virtues." Moses Almosnino, the eloquent Salonican rabbi, referred to her as "the Lady, crown of the glory of goodly women," the crusty Joshua Soncino, her opponent, as "the crowned Lady, chaplet of grace of the hosts of Israel . . . who built the house of Israel with holiness and purity with her wealth and treasure," going on to speak enthusiastically of her charitableness and her work for the succor of her oppressed coreligionists. The chronicler Samuel Usque described her in a dedication, in a much-quoted phrase, as: "the heart of her people," that being "the principal and noblest organ of the human body, feeling most readily the pain suffered by any other part," and foretold how her name and memory would remain engraved in the very bones of her coreligionists. "It ceased to be with this Lady after the manner of women," audaciously misquoted Saadiah Lungo, the poet-in-ordinary of the Salonican community. "Like a man, she girded her loins with might and strengthened her arms . . . making a name like unto the names of the great and holy ones. . . . Verily, there was the garment of a man on a woman." The learned Rabbi Moses di Trani summed up the opinion of his contemporaries, in a slight variation of the words of King Solomon: "Many daughters have done virtuously, but Hannah hath excelled them all."

The modern biographer, however cautious or even sceptical his approach may have been in the first instance, is impelled to confirm these opinions. After the most detailed investigation of every scrap of evidence relating to her career, he fails to find any stain, however trivial, on the nobility of her character, or any detail, however insignificant, calculated to modify the contemporary judgment. No other woman in Jewish history has been surrounded with such devotion and affection. No other woman in Jewish history, it seems, has deserved it more.

CHAPTER VII

The Ancona Boycott

PERHAPS the most dramatic episode in Doña Gracia Nasi's public life was her leadership in the attempt to avenge, by direct action, a terrible injury that had been inflicted on her coreligionists in Italy. It was she, the woman, who at this time provided the inspiration and the determination that was lacking among the men, and in connection with this her warm, eager nature is seen to best advantage. It is necessary, however, to prelude the story with a detailed account of the tragedy with which the episode began.

Among the cities in which the House of Nasi maintained a business agency was the ancient seaport of Ancona, halfway down the east (Adriatic) coast of Italy. During the Middle Ages this had been a nominal republic, but it had fallen not long since under the sway of the Popes, its liberties being soon suppressed. By way of compensation, its new masters determined to make it the commercial gateway to their dominions — indeed, to central Italy as a whole — thus diverting into their own coffers part of the golden stream that had hitherto been almost monopolized by Venice. It was impossible in such circumstances to pay jealous regard to the purity of faith; for Turkish merchants could not conceivably be shut out from a city the greatest part of whose trade lay with the Levant, and, if Moslems were admitted, it was illogical to exclude the Jews.

There had, indeed, been an old, indigenous Jewish colony there, since the thirteenth century at the latest, its most illustrious member being the satiric poet of this period, Immanuel of Rome, parodist and perhaps friend of Dante Alighieri. It still flourished; and very soon after the decisive papal occupation of the city under Pope Clement VII, Marrano refugees from Portugal also began to find their way thither, as they did to almost every other part of Italy. When his successor, Pope Paul III, declared Ancona a free port and cordially invited foreign merchants to settle there, the rights of non-Christians were specifically guaranteed, the Jews being, moreover, graciously exempted from excessive special taxation and from the obligation to wear any special badge or sign to distinguish them, in a contemptuous sense, from the rest of the population.

By now, the Inquisition had begun its activities in Portugal, and the New Christians were searching desperately for fresh havens of refuge. In the circumstances, Ancona naturally suggested itself; but it was obviously inadvisable to flock without special safeguards to a place which was under the hand and eye of the Popes themselves. Rome was not unreasonable in such matters, and delegates, amply supplied with money, were constantly there at this time on behalf of the Portuguese Marranos, to secure some restriction on the activities of the Holy Office at home. It was thanks probably to their efforts that the Pope issued an elaborate brief on February 21, 1547, encouraging New Christians from Portugal to share in the safe-conduct granted to foreign merchants

who frequented the port in question. Above all, he undertook that, in case of any accusation of heresy or apostasy,
they should be subject exclusively to the papal jurisdic-
tion, no subordinate judge or inquisitor being allowed
cognizance of the case.

Two years later, a group of Portuguese New Christians, headed by a couple of physicians, entered into an
agreement with the city to set up a loan-bank in order to
relieve the pressing needs of the poor. (This was regarded
in Italy at that time as a specific Jewish function and was
the original *raison dê'tre* of the communities of the center
and north of the country.) In return for this service, the
commune undertook to grant admission to thirty or
thirty-five Portuguese families; these were, moreover, to
be guaranteed from prosecution for any matter of faith
except before the Pope himself, and were promised
twelve months' grace to settle their affairs should action
be contemplated against them at any time on this score.
It was understood that approval of this arrangement
would be obtained from the Pope. Owing to Paul III's
death, there was some delay in this, but at the close of 1552
the terms of the agreement and of all previous concessions
were confirmed in the most solemn form by his successor,
Julius III. He too guaranteed the Portuguese who came
to Ancona against prosecution by any ecclesiastical court
for the practice of Judaism, whatever their religious antecedents might have been, though he reduced the period
of grace in which to settle their affairs in case of necessity
from twelve months to four. In the following year, he
confirmed and extended these concessions (March 20,
1553), exempting the Portuguese also, like the native
Jews, from the obligation to wear any distinguishing

badge and promising them that no attempt would be made to baptize their children against their will. They on their side undertook to pay him the sum of 1,000 ducats yearly on account of the *vigesima* (twentieth) and other ecclesiastical taxes. Outside Italy, the Pope's policy was presented in its most sordid light, and it was reported that he had succumbed to the temptation of sheer bribery. At the Council of Trent, the Portuguese delegate, the bishop of Oporto, had expressed bewilderment at the Supreme Pontiff's equivocal action in first encouraging his king to allow Marranos to emigrate freely and then permitting them to return to Judaism under his very eyes.

Under such favorable circumstances Ancona became a veritable city of refuge for the Portuguese New Christians. The immigrants organized themselves as a separate community (*universitas*). Within a few years it numbered something like one hundred households. A synagogue was established in a house rented from Messer Niccolò Gratioli, in which divine worship was conducted in accordance with the Portuguese tradition, which differed in some respects from that of the native Italian communities. Portuguese travellers, zealous for the faith, returning to Lisbon from abroad, recounted to the Holy Office how they had met there, professing Judaism openly, persons whom they themselves had formerly known at home as Christians. The economic hopes that had been placed in them were not disappointed, for they assisted in bringing about a remarkable revival of trade in the port, so that its quays were piled high with merchandise and the constant building hardly kept pace with the need for new dwellings and warehouses. More than one of the great Jewish mercantile houses of Italy and the Levant maintained agencies among them. The House of Abrabanel of Ferrara was represented by the polished, pious Solomon Jachia.[1] Doña Gracia Nasi herself had four factors — Jacob Mosso, Aman and Azim (Hayyim?) Cohen and Abraham Mus. It was probably on her business that her trusted associate, the litterateur and patron of letters Duarte Gomez, visited Ancona about this time. Here he was treated for an indisposition by the lifelong friend of the family, Amatus Lusitanus, who was also attracted by the extremely favorable conditions that prevailed and established a lucrative private practice, among which he culled the details of many of the fascinating case histories recorded in his classical *Centuriae Curationum*. Among his other patients was the governor of Ancona, through whose recommendation he was summoned to Rome to treat his uncle, Pope Julius III, shortly after his election in 1550. Another eminent local Marrano notable was his friend and competitor and at one time patient, Dr. Francisco Barboso, who had acquired riches and fame during a long residence in the Indies, the latter's clientèle also including the governor of the city and the prior of the local Dominican convent; while the Latin poet, Didaco Pyrrho (Diogo Pires), whom we have encountered already in Antwerp and Ferrara, was also in practice there. As we have seen, Doña Gracia and her family themselves probably stayed in the city for a while on their way from Ferrara to Turkey at the close of 1552 or the beginning of the next year.

On this prosperous little community, disaster suddenly fell, in what it was formerly possible to consider one of the most appalling tragedies in the whole course of Italian

Jewish history. (The events of 1943–5 have, alas, put
all such matters in an entirely different perspective.) Of
recent years Cardinal Giovanni Pietro Caraffa, in whom
the most fanatical aspects of the Counter-Reformation
were personified, had become more and more influential
in the Papal Curia and was now conducting a perpetual
anti-Jewish agitation. Already during the pontificate of
Julius III, he had been principally responsible for the
condemnation and public burning of Hebrew literature
in Rome and throughout the country, in the autumn of
1553. Not long after, in May, 1555, he himself ascended
the papal throne as Paul IV, determined to stem the
progress of the Reformation and religious disbelief wherever it might be encountered. Reaction was now triumphant. One of his first actions was to publish the
infamous Bull, *Cum nimis absurdum* ("Whereas it is
highly absurd"), which initiated the Ghetto system,
excluded the Jews from honorable walks of life, rigidly
enforced the wearing of the Jewish badge of shame, and
started the age of Jewish degradation that was to last in
Italy until the nineteenth century.[2] It was hardly to be
expected that he, inspirer of the campaign against the
Lutheran heretics, could complacently tolerate the presence in his own dominions of a colony of apostates to
Judaism who had once been Catholics. In a religious
issue he did not feel bound by the limitations accepted
by his predecessors. As we have seen, they had under-
taken time after time, in one solemn obligation after the
other, that the New Christians from Portugal living in
Ancona should not be subject to the Inquisitors or ordinary judges for prosecution in connection with any
matter of faith, and that if any proceedings were medi-

tated against them they should be allowed ample time to settle their affairs and withdraw. At the outset of the new pontificate, the Cardinal Carlo Caraffa, his beloved nephew, had confirmed this, at least by implication, when he renewed the privileges of the city. Notwithstanding this, in July, 1555, the Pope sent to Ancona a certain Giovanni Vincenzo Fallongonio, of Naples, as apostolic commissioner with plenary powers, in order to take proceedings against the Portuguese renegades who had abandoned the Christian faith into which they had been baptized (the circumstances were irrelevant) and had now returned to Judaism.

The papal representative acted with a vigor worthy of a far better cause. The whole of the Portuguese community in the city, as well as various individuals in outlying places — fully a hundred persons all told — were suddenly arrested and thrown into gaol, though a few were forewarned and managed to flee in time. Inquisitorial proceedings were opened against them forthwith. The victims made a vain attempt to secure a reprieve by offering a bribe of 50,000 ducats. But this was no vulgar piece of blackmail, as previously was so often the case. In a brief of October 1, the Pope forbade the commutation of any prosecution in return for monetary payment, at the same time ordering that any privileges invalidating the proceedings which might be produced by the accused should be torn up and treated as void.

It was in vain therefore that the prisoners appealed to the solemn guarantees that they had received from the city of Ancona and from successive Popes, safeguarding them in the most precise and comprehensive terms against any such onslaught as this. Their condition would have been even more desperate but for the fact that the commissary Fallongonio, as greedy as he was unprincipled, connived at the flight from gaol of one prisoner after the other. In the end, a remarkable coup was brought about, no fewer than thirty of them escaping together in a single batch. By the time this had become known, of course, he himself was no longer at hand to face the responsibility. The confiscations had placed under his control enormous quantities of money and precious merchandise. (The total value was estimated at 300,000 ducats.) What with this and the bribes he had received, he was in command of tremendous wealth, with which he had prudently absconded. (It was only in the following December that he was traced in Genoa, whence the Pope demanded his extradition from the doge and council.) But all did not escape. Upwards of fifty persons were left to the vengeance of the Pope; and a terrible vengeance it was.

The new commissary was Cesare della Nave[3] of Bologna, a man after the Pope's own heart — fanatical, pitiless, incorruptible. He pressed on with the prosecution unremittingly. So as to make further untoward episodes impossible, the prisoners were henceforth shackled to one another with iron chains. The proceedings against them followed the normal inquisitional method. In accordance with the spirit of the time, torture was lavishly used in order to extract the necessary evidence or "confessions." For greater effect, this was carried out in public; and merchants from the Levant, on their way through the streets, would suddenly be brought face to face with their unhappy coreligionists as they were dragged along in fetters to their examination or were submitted to the horrors of the *strappado* in the principal square of the city. They of course had, in fact, no legal defense. They had discarded Christianity and had openly lived in Ancona as Jews. It was indubitable, then, that they were renegades, and their fate under ecclesiastical law was as obvious as it was certain. Any who professed repentance and solemnly undertook to conduct themselves in future as faithful Christians might indeed be "reconciled" to the Holy Church and allowed to live. But for those who refused to abjure their newly-refound Judaism only one sentence was possible — death.

In the spring and summer of 1556, a series of "Acts of Faith" was held in the Campo della Mostra at Ancona, at which the unhappy victims appeared before the jeering crowd. Those who were ostensibly contrite performed a public act of penitence and abjuration and were sentenced to less severe punishments; the "contumacious," twenty-four in number, were handed over to the secular arm, for the execution of the capital penalty with which the Church could nominally have no direct association, first being strangled and then burned.[4]

They bore some of the most familiar names in the record of Spanish Jewry. (The high-sounding Marrano sobriquets by which they had once been known are unrecorded.) The first victims perished on April 13; they were the aged Doña Maiora (the only woman who figured in the entire group), Simeon ben Menahem, Samuel Guascon, Abraham Falcon and Joseph Oheb (possibly, Amatus Lusitanus' brother.)[5] Two days later, the spectacle was repeated, the sufferers on this occasion being Isaac Nahmias and Solomon Aguades. The next day came the turn of Moses Pajo, Solomon Finto, Joseph

Molcho, Abraham Cirilio, David Nahash and Abraham Spagna (="of Spain").

At this point, there was a brief intermission, for some of the prisoners tried to escape their fate by maintaining steadfastly, even under repeated torture, that they had never been baptized and hence were not subject to the Inquisition, any more than other Jews faithful to their creed. This presented the tribunal with something of a juridical problem, for they had never lived in Italy as Christians and it was hence impossible to produce positive evidence of their baptism. A "Congregation" held in Rome in April ended the perplexity by deciding that no attention should be paid to this plea, as it was notorious that no unbaptized Jew had been allowed to live in Portugal for the past sixty years. Hence the necessity for technical evidence on this point was dispensed with, and on June 15 and 20 the capital sentences were delivered at two further Acts of Faith. The victims on the former occasion were Joseph Barzillon, the boy David Reuben, Solomon Jachia, David Sacriario, Joseph Vardai, Joseph Pappo, Jacob Cohen and Jacob Montalban: and on the latter Abraham Lobo ("the foremost of the second band," in the poet's words), the venerable Abraham Cohen, and Jacob Mosso, the local agent of Doña Gracia Nasi's business house.

Down to the very end, the martyrs withstood the temptation to save their lives by professing Christianity again. On their way, still shackled, to the place of execution (it was afterwards recounted) those who knew Italian assured the bystanders that they died gladly for the sake of the One God. Solomon Jachia above all (he was the Abrabanels' factor and had a fine command of language) addressed those who had come to enjoy the spectacle and told them how it was for the Unity of the God of Israel that he laid down his life. Afterwards, he recited in a loud voice the benediction prescribed by tradition for those about to undergo martyrdom: *"Blessed art Thou, our God, King of the Universe, Who hast sanctified us by Thy commandments and bidden us to sanctify Thy name."* He then sprang spontaneously into the flames, spurning the mercy of preliminary strangulation. One of the prisoners, seeing no hope of escape, and fearing that he might not have sufficient fortitude to hold out to the end, had committed suicide by throwing himself out of the window of his cell, the Jews being permitted to bury his body in their cemetery. Thus the total number of victims was brought up to twenty-five.[6]

Several Hebrew elegies were written commemorating the holocaust and perpetuating the identity and the heroism of the victims — by Jacob da Fano, Solomon Hazan, Mordecai di Blanes, and others — some of them being adopted into the liturgy of local synagogues for recital on the Ninth of Ab, the fast-day commemorating the destruction of Jerusalem.[7] These are among the most moving productions of Italian Jewish literature of the sixteenth century. Especially affecting is one by an anonymous writer, composed in the form of a vision of Paradise, in a vaguely Dantesque tradition. In this, the martyrs are introduced one by one and recount in pathetic words how they had been purified by the flame which brought them near to God's presence, where they would enjoy bliss for ever; and they advise those whom they left behind on earth to observe without flinching the

Divine Law, source of everlasting life, and to look forward steadfastly to the great Day of Deliverance.

In the nineteenth century there was a curious sequel. The tragic happenings at Ancona were recounted in more than one Hebrew chronicle of the period. The martyrs were commemorated in the local synagogues year by year. They were, as we have seen, mourned in a number of elegies by contemporary poets. There were many subsidiary notices. Nevertheless, a tender-hearted Catholic historian, unable to believe that the Church could be guilty of such horrors, denied the veracity of the entire story and published a monograph in 1876 in order to disprove the "alleged" Act of Faith held at Ancona under Pope Paul IV.[8] Since then, yet further evidence has accumulated; and though the actual record of the trials has not yet been discovered, it is impossible nowadays to question seriously the historicity of this agonizing episode.

Those who had been "reconciled" at the public Acts of Faith, having professed repentance, numbered thirty-eight.[9a] As their punishment, or penance (in fact the two could not be distinguished except by the exercise of considerable intellectual subtlety), twenty-six[9b] of them were condemned to the galleys, being sent to Malta, clad in the green-yellow robes of contrition[10] which they were supposed to wear for many years, to row in the predatory vessels of the Knights of St. John. On the way they managed to overcome their guards — it is not known how — and to escape to some place where they could hope for greater tolerance — some to Ferrara, some to Turkey — where they re-embraced Judaism as before. Only one person of the entire New Christian corporation

is recorded to have been treated more tenderly. This was
Amatus Lusitanus' friend, Dr. Barboso. Owing to his
services to the people of Ancona, including the papal
commissary himself, he was released after his formal
reconciliation and allowed to resume his medical practice,
though handicapped by his ridiculous penitential robe.
In due course he made his way to Salonica where he too
reverted to the public profession of Judaism.[11] (His wife
had preceded him, being smuggled out of prison by a
Jewish attendant.) Amatus himself, the most distinguished physician perhaps of his age, had a narrow
escape. Orders had been issued for his arrest, his house
had been entered and his property and library sequestered — including the fifth book of his famous case
histories and his commentary on Avicenna. Owing to
the efforts of his friends, the former was subsequently
recovered from the papal commissary, but the commentary was lost forever. He himself was apparently
forewarned of what was about to happen; in any case, he
managed to make his way, unmolested, to Pesaro, where
he continued his former life and work. The exercise of
force was sufficient to enforce hypocrisy or concealment·
it could not make a man change his convictions.

In the autumn of 1555, the first reports of the arrests
in Ancona reached Doña Gracia Nasi in Constantinople,
earlier probably than anyone else. She was horrified.
The victims were her kith and kin. She had helped many
of them to escape from Portugal; with some of them she
had become personally acquainted perhaps when she
passed through Ancona; among their number were her
own trusted agents and correspondents. From the point

SILVER DOORS OF THE ARK IN THE "ITALIAN"
SYNAGOGUE OF ANCONA

A Turkish Jewish Merchant in Italy

of view of Church Law, of course — and therefore of civil
law in the Papal States — their position was indefensible.
But there was a higher code — the code of humanity.
It was a code which in the course of the nineteenth century prompted the western powers on more than one
occasion to intervene with the "backward" countries
of the Moslem East on behalf of their persecuted Jewish
subjects — an action which was possible and sometimes
successful because they were the stronger. At that time,
in the sixteenth century, the pictures were reversed. The
greatest military power of the age was Turkey, as yet at
the height of her reputation; and Turkish policy was
tolerant, liberal and humane to a degree in comparison
with that of Christian Europe, where those who would
not conform to the established religion of the state were
burned, massacred, harried and placed outside the bounds
of ordinary society. Hence at this period Turkey filled
much the same position in international politics, from
this point of view, as England did in the nineteenth century. Thanks to the efforts of certain influential and
warm-hearted Jews who played a part in public life in
Constantinople, the Ottoman empire assumed a quasi-
protectorate (in its most literal sense) over downtrodden
Jews elsewhere; seeking excuses for intervention on their
behalf, on the most trivial pretext, whenever it was possible. There was an instance of this, as we have seen,
when, ostensibly on the grounds that Doña Gracia Nasi
and her family intended to settle in Turkey, the sultan
professed to regard them as his subjects *in posse* and
demanded their release from the Venetian republic. In
the present instance there was, indeed, a more plausible
excuse. Some of the persons arrested had been domiciled

in Turkey and might thus be considered Turkish nationals in the technical sense; others represented Turkish firms and could claim Turkish protection on that account. Moreover, in the course of the wholesale confiscations which accompanied the arrests, a great deal of property belonging to other Jews who were indubitably Ottoman subjects had also been casually seized; debts owed by others to the prisoners had been vigorously exacted, but no payment had been allowed to anyone on account of what they themselves owed; Levantine merchants who arrived in the city, or who were forced to put into port owing to unfavorable winds, found themselves molested on the suspicion of being of Marrano origin; while the Turkish Jewish traders, who were unfortunate enough to have merchandise deposited with their coreligionists in Ancona, lost everything. The rabbis of Constantinople and Salonica found themselves confronted in the next few months with perplexing problems of law arising out of the sudden disruption of trade.[12] Many wealthy firms were thus reduced to poverty. The total loss to Ottoman subjects — and indirectly to the Ottoman exchequer — was very considerable indeed. The sultan was not, therefore, unwilling to have an excuse for exerting his influence· After receiving Doña Gracia Nasi in personal audience, and listening to her heart-rending story (so at least the contemporary Jewish chronicler states)[13] he sent a special envoy to Ancona demanding the release of all those prisoners who were Turkish-protected subjects and threatening reprisals if his request were not complied with.

On the receipt of this communication, in December, the Ancona merchants became fearful for their trade and hastily despatched the "Magnificent" Giulio de Bonibus to Rome on an urgent special mission. He was instructed to seek an audience with the Pope, in the company of their permanent representative, Monsignor Pietro Leoni, and to make their quandary clear. Of course, they could not but praise his Holiness' determination to eradicate from their city these Marranos and Jewish apostates. But the slowness of the proceedings, coupled with the general uncertainty that had resulted from the first Commissary's flight, had been most disturbing for trade — especially as so much of the sequestered property belonged to Turkish Jews or was claimed by non-Jewish merchants. In consequence, ships and cargoes originally destined for Ancona were being diverted to Venice; indeed, it was suspected that the new governor of the city, Monsignore di Loreto, who was of Venetian origin, was deliberately trying to ruin their trade, with this in view. As a result of the Turkish intervention, grave risks were incurred in the Levant not only by the Ancona traders but by all those from the Papal States. It was imperative, they concluded, that something should be done about all this as soon as possible. At the very least the trials of the Portuguese infidels should be transferred to Macerata, or some other inland town in the neighborhood, so as to prevent the foreign Jewish merchants who frequented the port, and were responsible for so much of its trade, from being terrorized by the sight of their coreligionists as they were dragged through the streets for public torture. It was perfectly obvious that the city hoped to achieve, at all events, something which would minimize abroad the impression of their personal complicity.[14]

No attention whatsoever was paid by the Pope to

these petitions: for (as we have seen) the trials proceeded
as hitherto. However the sultan may have felt inclined
at this stage, we may be sure that Doña Gracia gave no
opportunity for the matter to pass into oblivion at Constantinople and saw that it was kept before his attention.
At the beginning of March, the grand vizier, Rustam
Pasha, Joseph Nasi's bosom friend, sent for the consul
designate for Ancona and informed him that his master
strongly resented what was happening in Italy, which
had already cost him a direct loss of 400,000 ducats. He
now peremptorily demanded the release without delay
of all those of the prisoners who were in the employment
of Turkish residents and thus were technically Turkish
protected subjects — above all the agents of Doña
Gracia Nasi, who (he said) normally resided in Constantinople and were in Ancona only on a visit. If this
were not done, he threatened immediate reprisals. A
letter to the same effect was written simultaneously to
the governor of Ancona, expressing indignation at the
fact that no reply had been received to the communication sent some months before, and asking that Doña
Gracia's agents and their property should be placed in
the charge of her ubiquitous representatives, Duarte
Gomez and Agostino Enriques.[15] In case this request of
the Ottoman government was not complied with at once,
steps would be taken to make her losses good out of the
property of the Ancona merchants trading in the Levant.
To show that this was meant seriously, orders were issued
for impounding at once all vessels in Turkish waters
which belonged to citizens of that place. Nor was this
by any means all. The Florentine *bailo* in Constantinople
was requested somewhat peremptorily to see what he

could do in the matter. What was more important, Michel de Codignac, ambassador in Turkey for the French king (who was traditionally regarded as protector of the Christians in the Near East), was also desired to use his good offices, in view of the serious international repercussions which might result if the dispute were to drift any further. He considered the commission to be of such extreme importance that he despatched Baron Pierre Cochard, secretary of the embassy, to Italy in a last attempt to smooth matters over. With him the latter carried a letter on the subject from the sultan himself, and addressed this time to His Holiness the Pope in person, almost in the form of an ultimatum — a unique document of its kind, which attracted much attention at the time among the general public and was included by the litterateur, Girolamo Ruscelli, in his famous "Collection of Princely Letters."[16] It embodied much the same demands in a form only slightly more diplomatic:

Suleiman the Sultan, Great Emperor of all other Emperors, son of Sultan Selim, likewise Emperor over all other Emperors, Whom may God cause to triumph eternally: to the High and Mighty Lord of the Generation of the Messiah Jesus, Prince and Lord of Rome: May the Great God preserve you!

When you shall have received my Divine and Imperial Seal, which will be presented to you, you must know that certain persons of the race of the Jews have informed my Elevated and Sublime Porte that, whereas certain subjects and tributaries of Ours have gone to your territories to traffic, and especially to Ancona, their goods and property have been seized on your instructions. This is in particular to the prejudice of Our Treasury, to the amount of 400,000 ducats, over and above the damage done to Our subjects, who have been ruined and cannot pay their obligations to Our said Treasury, on account of the customs-duties and commerce of Our ports, which they had in their hands.[16a] We therefore request Your Holiness, that by virtue of this Our universal and illustrious Seal, which will be brought to you by the secretary Cachard, a man in the service of the Most High and Magnanimous King, Prince of Princes of the said generation of the Messiah Jesus, the most Christian Majesty of the King of France, our very dear friend, you will be pleased to liberate our above-mentioned ... subjects, with all the property which they had and owned, in order that they may be able to satisfy their debts, and the above-mentioned customs officials will no longer excuse their failure to pay by reason of the retention of the said prisoners. By so doing, you will give Us occasion to treat in friendly fashion your subjects and the other Christians who traffic in these parts.

In full confidence that you will so do, we will say no more to Your Holiness, except, that God prosper you for many years.

Given in Our fortunate Imperial seat, the last day of the blessed moon of Rambelachi, in the year of the prophet 964 [March 9, 1556].

In addition to this peremptory document, Cochard brought with him a personal letter from the ambassador to the Duke di Pagliano, the Pope's all-powerful nephew (none could at that time foretell the gruesome fate that awaited him) who was expected to be able to exercise a moderating influence.

The special envoy, bearing the despatches and communications from Constantinople, reached Italy only at the end of April, after the first batch of executions had taken place. On receiving the sultanic missive, the city council of Ancona, more alarmed now than ever, once again sent a special representative to present their case before the Pope. But the latter, intent as ever on purifying his dominions from the taint of Marranism, remained obdurate, not only to this, but even to more influential representations. He deigned to reply to the sultan; but his letter (dated June 1, 1556) was almost a model of epistolary bigotry. He was prepared, he said, as a personal favor to his fellow-sovereign, to give orders for the release of those prisoners who were Turkish subjects and who could not be proved to have professed Christianity at any time, even if other charges had peradventure been brought against them; and the Baron de Cochard was asked to escort them and their property back to Turkey — a charge which he prudently refused, having decided that it was a good deal more pleasant to dally in Venice and conduct all negotiations by correspondence. In addition, the property which had been in the hands of Doña Gracia's agents was released from embargo, as a friendly gesture to the Grand Signior. The latter was assured, moreover, that, if his Jewish subjects were guilty of no offense from the point of view of Christianity, they would continue to be well treated; the recent creation of a ghetto in Ancona being somewhat preposterously adduced in proof of this. But as regards the main issue, the Pope would not budge. Those New Christians who had reverted to Judaism must suffer for it; and he refused to pardon even Jacob Mosso, Doña Gracia's personal agent, concerning whose Marrano antecedents there was no possibility at all of doubt.[17] All this was reaffirmed by his nephew, the Duke di Pagliano, in his letter of reply of June 6 to the French ambassador to Turkey. That very day eight more of the victims were burned in Ancona; just under a week later, the last three, including Jacob Mosso, met the same fate.

The sultan had done what he could. But, since the Pope had agreed to confine his action within the limits of international law, it was hardly possible for him to press the matter any further. Moreover, the tragedy had reached its climax. It was now too late for prevention or for protection. But it was not too late for revenge.

When the onslaught at Ancona began, some of the Marrano element, warned in time, had taken refuge in the duchy of Urbino — the only neighboring state where they could reasonably hope for safety. Above all, they were attracted by the seaport of Pesaro, some thirty-seven miles to the north, at the estuary of the river Foglia, the physician Amatus Lusitanus being among those who fixed their residence there. The reigning duke, Guidubaldo II della Rovere, was by no means displeased. He was doing his utmost to develop the commerce of his little duchy which centered on this place, having not long since removed his capital thither from the inland hill-town of Urbino. There was, indeed, an old-established indigenous Jewish community there, but the advent of the Portuguese element with their influential connections overseas seemed to hold the promise of exceptional economic advantages. Hence, when the Marranos had been driven from Ferrara during the plague of 1551, an older settler, one Manuel Bichaco, had induced him to admit some of them, Pope Paul III raising no objections. Thus there was already at Pesaro a Portuguese community also, with its own synagogue, which some irrepressible rowdies (headed by the duke's brother) had desecrated a year or so before in a drunken prank. The happenings in the Papal States held out the promise of more dramatic, more lucrative developments. What if the fugitives should succeed in bringing with them the Levantine commerce formerly centered at Ancona, so that Pesaro took its place as the principal port of the middle Adriatic and the maritime gateway to Central Italy? They confidently assured the duke that they would bring this about, and on this understanding he opened his duchy freely to

them, even going so far as to refuse a demand of the
Pope's for their extradition. But it was impossible for
the handful of fugitives to achieve what they promised
by themselves, unaided. They needed the collaboration
of their coreligionists in the Levant, who all but controlled
the trade of the Turkish empire. It was in their hands
to demonstrate Jewish solidarity for once in a practical
manner and to show that it was possible to avenge an
outrage as well as to deplore it. And the Marranos at
Pesaro, their tenacity enhanced by their desire for vengeance, set themselves to the task of arousing their feelings
of responsibility.

Their agent was one of the Ancona fugitives who had
managed to escape with his life — "a brand plucked from
the burning," as he was described — named Judah Faraj.
On the very day that the pyre was lit at Ancona, in
April, 1556, he was sent as their emissary to the Levant,
notwithstanding his now-precarious health. With him
he bore a letter (couched for safety's as well as for learning's sake in highly cryptic style), which recounted the
details of the grim tragedy that had taken place and
suggested the method of revenge. Now was the time for
the Jews throughout the world to arouse themselves, and
to show that (in the rabbinic phrase) "all Israel were
sureties the one for the other." Let no man trade with
the city of blood, not even to the extent of a single copper;
let no merchant visit the place, no cargo be consigned to
it, no ship be directed thither. The Turks, too, might be
persuaded to collaborate, for the Sultanic Majesty had
also been offended. The city of Ancona would lie desolate and ruined, a monument to the criminal folly of the
Pope's barbaric action; and the duke of Urbino would

be rewarded for his generous offer of asylum by seeing his port of Pesaro flourish as never before.

All this was further elaborated by Judah Faraj by word of mouth, first at Salonica, where support was unanimous and enthusiastic, and then at Constantinople. Here he certainly found a warm and sympathetic welcome at the Nasi mansion from Doña Gracia and her nephew, desperate at the fate that had overtaken their Ancona associates and needing no encouragement for further action.

At a meeting held at Constantinople in July, 1556 — presumably under their auspices — Faraj's tragic story brought tears to the eyes of those who participated, including some of the most distinguished rabbinical and lay leaders of the Turkish empire. It was determined to proclaim a boycott of the port of Ancona, to last for eight months, until the Passover of the following year, when a further general assembly would be held to decide whether or not it was to be continued. Meanwhile, all merchandise formerly consigned by Jewish merchants throughout Turkey to the guilty port was to be despatched to Pesaro instead, under penalty of excommunication. Doña Gracia on her side supported the scheme warmly. Not content with setting the example, by transferring all her business to Pesaro, she communicated with the rabbis and scholars throughout the Ottoman dominions, desiring them to support the scheme and to associate their communities with the boycott by launching an excommunication against those who should infringe it. On the whole, they were compliant, from considerations of personal interest perhaps no less than of conviction. The Grand Signior looked on benignly; indeed, on another occasion, he himself placed an embargo on the port of Ancona in order to oblige the Venetians, during an interlude of amity with that Power, and the Pope's treatment of his subjects did not predispose him to act benevolently at present.

The consequences could soon be felt at Ancona. There were numerous bankruptcies among the merchants. Raw products of Turkish origin, such as skins and metals, rose steeply in price; the bales of cloth formerly exported were piled high in the warehouses and on the wharves. The city fathers, now thoroughly alarmed, wrote a pathetic appeal to the Pope on August 10 telling him of the information that had reached them and of the desperate straits to which they were being reduced, and imploring immediate succor. The Marranos at Pesaro on their side sent a second letter to their Levantine coreligionists congratulating them on what had already been achieved to "break the arms of the wicked who live in the City of Blood, in whose skirts is the blood of our martyrs," and encouraging them to fresh efforts. Should any difficulty arise, or any new facilities be required, they were prepared to make representations to the duke, who would certainly listen favorably in view of the fact that his port was now on its way to becoming a great harbor and an important center of international trade.

It appeared, for the moment, as though the Jews were about to carry out with success something which had been hardly known hitherto in the history of the Diaspora — a response to physical outrage not only by fasting and prayer, nor by the turning of the other cheek, which they alone practiced though they alone in Europe did not preach it; but by a vigorous, systematic, calculated exercise of pressure in the only field in which they had the slightest power. As the bills of lading for the vessels sailing in the name of Doña Gracia and her house were made out for Pesaro, and the merchandise formerly destined for Ancona was diverted to the rival port, it seemed to her as though her agent, Jacob Mosso, together with his associates, were in some slight measure avenged. It was an episode the like of which was not to be known again in Jewish history for another four centuries, until the attempt of the Jews to organize a boycott of German goods and services after the rise of the Nazis to power at the beginning of the antisemitic outrages in Germany in 1933.

Unhappily, even at this point and in such a matter, there was no unanimity, then as well. A boycott such as this was obviously ineffectual unless it was universal; in fact, the Salonica merchants had accepted it at the very outset only on condition that it was joined in by those of Constantinople, Adrianople and Brusa, in Asia Minor, then the fourth trading city of the Ottoman empire. Though a few individuals there demurred, the Jews of Constantinople were not backward, as we have seen, if only because of the authority of the House of Nasi. Those of Adrianople followed suit. The community of Brusa, on the other hand, held back, on the pretext that the material interests involved were too great, the port of Pesaro being inadequately equipped for handling a large volume of trade. (There had, it seems, been some serious accidents at the outset because of this.) Thus, owing to their opposition, the boycott was never really universal from the very first, and in the long run the result of this was to prove disastrous. Another side to the question, moreover, was now beginning to receive attention. Ancona was not after all a self-contained political entity, nor did its Marrano community comprise all of the local Jewish residents. There was in addition the old established, indigenous "Italian" group, which had already been settled there for some three centuries, mainly engaged in petty commerce and loan-banking. If Ancona were ruined, they would be ruined too; what was more, if Ancona were ruined by the Jews of the Levant, the inhabitants — and the Pope — would avenge themselves on the Jews of the locality. However sweet revenge might be, it could only be achieved at their cost — and the cost would not be light at such a time, when the terrible Pontiff was engaged in pressing home his offensive against the Jews.

The rabbi at Ancona at that time was the aged Moses Bassola — the same who had taken up arms a few years before in favor of the publication of the *Zohar*, the great Jewish mystical classic. He was by no means unacquainted with the Levantine world, for as a young man he had gone on pilgrimage to Palestine, his account of which (published indeed in full only in our own day) was a guide both to its sacred sites and to its economic potentialities. (Later on, he was to return to spend his last days there, dying in the Holy City of Safed in 1560, very shortly after his arrival.) It was on him that his flock relied to present their case and to take action on their behalf. Supported by two prominent Levantine merchants established in Ancona, Samuel Senior and Moses Jarhi, he now appealed to his colleagues in Turkey in a circular letter begging them to have pity on the remnant of his community; if they would not withdraw their excommunication on those members of their flocks who traded with that port, he said persuasively, they should at least allow every city to decide its policy for itself.

The Turkish rabbis were now divided into two opposing camps. On the whole, those of Spanish origin, who were especially concerned with the fate of the Marranos and incidentally were most obviously under the influence of the House of Nasi, considered that the boycott should be maintained. On the other hand, the important minority who belonged to the Italian or German or autochthonous Greek elements tended to think in more conventional terms and to consider the interests of those Jews left in Ancona to be paramount. From this point a considerable proportion of the less determined among the Turkish merchants began to waver. Even at Salonica, where the boycott proposals had been so generously approved at the outset, some members of the community now pleaded that they had given their assent under pressure, and that non-adhesion of the Brusa community automatically implied the cancellation of the agreement. A certain Solomon Bonsenior and his agent, Joseph Hodara, made themselves notorious as blockade-runners, not only disregarding the boycott themselves but encouraging others to entrust consignments to them. The quays of Ancona began to return to life.

The new development profoundly alarmed the Pesaro merchants. They had been admitted by the duke, not because of his personal feeling of benevolence, but on the definite understanding that they would divert the Levantine trade from Ancona. If they failed to carry out their undertaking, there was no doubt that he would be avenged on them — it was enough for him to allow ecclesiastical

law to take its course or to agree to the Pope's demand
for the extradition of the fugitives. The collapse of the
boycott might mean, not merely their ruin, but their
destruction. Hence a new factor came into consideration. It was not only a question of revenge on Ancona,
but, at this stage, of their own safety; and discussions in
the Levant turned more and more about this point,
which the opponents of the embargo systematically
minimized. The Ancona merchants on their side maintained that the duke of Urbino was á wise and good man,
so that the refugees would stand in no danger even if their
undertaking were not carried out — or, alternatively,
that he was at the bottom anti-Jewish, and deserved no
consideration; that he would consider himself sufficiently
rewarded if he secured for his dominions the trade of
those Marranos who did not now dare to venture to
Ancona; that the continuation of the boycott would
entail terrible consequences for the Jews of the Papal
States as a whole, exposed to the Pope's vengeance; and
that Pesaro, in addition to lacking facilities for handling
large quantities of merchandise, was plague-stricken.
Their rivals retorted that the inhabitants of Ancona were
notoriously unreliable, not to say mendacious; that
Pesaro in fact had not been visited by the plague, though
it had raged deplorably elsewhere; and that the duke was
prepared to go to great expense to improve the harbor
facilities, so that there was no likelihood of any further
untoward occurrences as in the past. In order to encourage customers, they were prepared to offer exceptionally attractive credit terms: not that this was really
necessary, for the consignments that had already arrived
had been sold before they were unloaded, or snatched

from the hands of the wholesalers by eager purchasers from many nations. As for the Pope, he had obviously determined to ruin the Jews of his dominions and required no further pretext. It was no longer, so far as they were concerned, a question of reprisals but of life and death for themselves, if owing to the supineness of their coreligionists they found themselves exposed to the resentment of the duke. They accordingly implored pitifully for a renewal of the embargo, coupled with punitive action against those who had infringed it; and they appealed especially to that tried sustainer of every Jewish cause, Doña Gracia Nasi. Meanwhile, Passover approached, and the eight-month period originally fixed for the boycott was drawing to a close. The communities of Salonica, Adrianople, Avlona and the Morea wrote to the capital requesting a prompt decision as to whether or not it was to be renewed. The success of the project was in the balance.

It was at this stage that Doña Gracia Nasi received the pathetic appeal of the Marranos of Pesaro. Her great Jewish heart was stirred. In view of the scale of her commercial operations and the magnitude of her commitments in Italy, she risked more by the boycott scheme than anyone else. But the implications had by now gone far beyond the original issue. She and her son-in-law, in advance of their age, realized the possibility of ameliorating the position of the Jews throughout the world, not by the twin traditional methods, of prayer and payment, but by direct political and economic action. (The present was not the only illustration of the fact.) This presupposed the existence among the Jews of a certain degree of discipline and cohesion, in default of which the eco-

nomic weapon was blunted and political action ludicrous.
If the undertaking made to the duke of Urbino were not
fulfilled, it would become obvious to the entire world
that the much-vaunted Jewish solidarity was a shadow,
and that however punctual Jews might be as individuals
in fulfilling their engagements no understanding could
possibly be arrived at with the Jews as a whole, whatever
their leading figures or self-appointed representatives
might promise.

Accordingly, Doña Gracia now made a supreme effort.
As a result of her intervention in the discussions, a fresh
conference of the foremost scholars and communal leaders
of the capital was now summoned to meet in the principal
Talmud Torah, or Public School, where public assemblies
were generally held. Here they were addressed once
again (of course, in Spanish) by Judah Faraj, the delegate
of the Pesaro community, who alleged that the Ancona
merchants were thinking only about their economic
interests, exaggerating their own dangers and minimizing
those of their neighbors. He proposed the appointment
of a sub-committee of five to investigate the question —
not (he said) because he was sanguine at this stage about
the possibilities of agreement, but because he desired his
efforts and arguments to be on record. His suggestion
was approved, but nothing resulted. (His enemies alleged
that this was because the nominees were impartial, and
were therefore expected to decide against him!) Faraj
meanwhile attempted to secure the adhesion of some of
the most eminent of the local scholars to a manifesto in
favor of the boycott, which emphasized the potentially
dangerous state of affairs at Pesaro while paying no attention whatsoever to the crisis of the Ancona community.

This procedure had the approval of Gracia Nasi and her son-in-law; and Rabbi Joseph ibn Leb, whose position as head of her academy made him almost her domestic chaplain, canvassed his colleagues in their name asking for signatures. Abraham Jerushalmi, rabbi of the Greek community in Constantinople and editor of the liturgy according to that rite (Venice, 1522), was induced to give his adhesion on his deathbed; other signatories included Rabbis Solomon Bilia and Solomon Saba.

Ibn Leb now approached Joshua Soncino, rabbi of the Great Synagogue, or Sinagoga Mayor, one of the oldest places of worship in the capital, which had existed even before the Turkish conquest. The latter was of Italian extraction, being descended from the famous family of printers who played so great a role in Hebrew and general typography in the fifteenth and sixteenth centuries, whose last representatives are known to have settled in Turkey.[18] His antecedents perhaps led him to resent the Sephardic hegemony in Turkish Jewry, and to think preponderantly of the interests of the geographical nucleus to which he traced his origin. When in the previous year the first meeting of the Constantinople rabbis had been summoned to consider the boycott, he had indeed been deeply impressed and at first had been whole-heartedly in favor of it. By now, however, he had changed his attitude, coming to the conclusion that the embargo was not only politically inadvisable, but from the talmudic standpoint actually illegal for various reasons. (It is conceivable of course that personal jealousy of Ibn Leb had entered into the question.) Communications from Salonica encouraged him in this attitude and he accordingly refused to sign the manifesto when he was approached.

The Nasi family was unaccustomed to such opposition, and one day he found himself summoned to the Nasi mansion together with two lay leaders of his synagogue, Solomon de Toledo and Abraham ibn Shushan. They were received by Don Joseph, greatly pressed for time, as he had to leave for Adrianople after the Court that same day. The latter (who considered himself the more qualified to judge the issue since he knew the duke of Urbino personally) somewhat peremptorily ordered the rabbi to append his name to the document. The other replied that he would do so only conditionally, with the reservation that he approved of it only if, as was alleged, there might actually be physical danger for the fugitives at Pesaro should the boycott be discontinued. When Nasi objected to this condition, the other stipulated as an alternative that, while signing, he should be allowed to inform his correspondents in Salonica that his assent was conditional. "Then do nothing at all," said the magnate; and he hurriedly left for his journey.

Doña Gracia was less likely to allow herself to be gainsaid. A few days later she sent for Moses di Segura, the president of the Sinagoga Mayor, and requested him to secure the recalcitrant rabbi's signature. A meeting of the congregation was held, and it was decided that he with five of the leading members (one of them being the wealthy poet-scholar Meir ibn Sanche, who enjoyed great influence in the city) should wait upon the *Señora* and explain his objections. He is the only person recorded to have braved the redoubtable matriarch, whom he now begged not to press him to act against his convictions,

especially as Don Joseph had signified approval of his
attitude. She replied, grimly, that however satisfied her
son-in-law might be, she was not. It was in vain that he
quoted edifying talmudic anecdotes in support of his
point of view, told her of conversations with Italian merchants who were familiar with local conditions, and
emphasized certain inconsistencies in the stories put
about by the supporters of the boycott. (It had been
reported for example that, because of his pro-Jewish
action, the duke had lost his position as Captain General
of the Church which he had held since 1550, and the considerable emoluments attached — a very misleading half-
truth, for this had happened in the normal course of
events on the death of the old Pope.) The interview was
obviously a stormy one, and the two parted without
reaching any agreement.

Now the grand tussle began, Doña Gracia becoming
more and more determined, Rabbi Joshua more and more
stubborn. He suggested that a special messenger should
be sent to Venice and Padua at his expense (he did not
intimate that some merchants who sympathized were
willing to pay their share) to enquire the view of such
Jewish notables and scholars as Meir Katzenellenbogen,
the venerated rabbi of the latter place, who might be
presumed to know the circumstances. But the matter was
too urgent to brook delay — even had the persons in question not belonged in the main to the German element,
who were least interested and in consequence had shown
themselves from the very outset antagonistic to the idea.

While the arguments were in progress, it became known
in Constantinople that the boycott party had stolen a
march on their opponents. Doña Gracia was not accus-

tomed to be thwarted and the opposition, after all, was not on such a scale that it was in her opinion necessary to take it overseriously. Her dependents had accordingly asked the Sephardi rabbis of the capital to proclaim the embargo in their own places of worship, as though it had been universally accepted. This was now done with the utmost solemnity, under pain of excommunication in case of disobedience, in two of the most important synagogues of the city — that of the Castilian Exile (*K. K. Gerush*) and that of the Portuguese, who were naturally the most interested. Though these were the most important of the Sephardi communities, the other eight are alleged to have hesitated to declare themselves; it was the first time in living memory that there had been any difference between them on a major issue.

It now became a matter of supreme importance for each of the two opposing factions to secure the adhesion of the non-Spanish minority in the Jewish community of the capital. Chance played at the outset into the hands of the boycott party. Owing to a communal split some time before, there were two small local synagogues following the German (Ashkenazi) rite, each with its own separate organization. The two rabbis had recently quarreled, and one of them appealed for assistance to Doña Gracia and her son-in-law, upon whom he waited one day together with various members of his community. Don Joseph considered this an admirable opportunity to persuade them to accept the embargo. They were all the more inclined to agree since it did not affect them overclosely; but they were prevented by a certain Joseph Ashkenazi, the only member of the community who traded with Ancona, who happened by chance to be one of the delegation. Don Joseph was thrown into a towering rage — all the more so since the rabbi's only visible means of sustenance was the daily allowance of thirty *aspri*[19] which he received as a member of Doña Gracia's *Yeshiba* or rabbinical academy. He told them forthrightly that if they persisted in their attitude, against his and his aunt's will, they could not expect to continue to enjoy their bounty; and immediately afterwards gave instructions that the allowance should be suspended. This brought the congregation to a sober sense of reality; and one day, when Joseph Ashkenazi was absent from the synagogue, they too proclaimed the boycott. Nasi would have preferred them to repeat the procedure more formally on a subsequent occasion, but gave up the idea on being informed that the other party would then have voiced its opposition in public. But he was now mollified, and the recalcitrant rabbi was presumably readmitted into favor.[20]

Thus, the Castilian, Portuguese and German communities had officially endorsed the embargo, and the boy-cott party seemed very near to success. Rabbi Joseph ibn Leb now approached the Byzantine Synagogue, the oldest of all, reminding them how their rabbi had subscribed on his deathbed to his original manifesto, and asking them to do the same. They acceded to his request — not unnaturally, sneered critics, seeing that none of them traded with Ancona, so that originally it had seemed unnecessary to invite their collaboration at all.

Victory for the policy seemed so probable at this stage that the opposition could no longer afford to hold its hand. Those merchants interested in Italian trade, who were antagonistic to the embargo, now encouraged Rabbi

Soncino to come out into the open. He accordingly issued a closely-argued legal document in which he attempted to demonstrate that the communal ordinance in favor of the boycott had no validity in Jewish law, both because of the method in which agreement had been secured and because of the talmudic principle that a man must not protect himself at another's expense. At the most it bound only the members of the communities which had adopted it, not others; he went even so far as to imply that the scholars who supported it were influenced only by sordid considerations, and that he had himself been threatened with serious consequences if he continued to maintain his opposition. With a notable lack of proportion, he called attention to the outrage that had taken place in the synagogue at Pesaro itself, not so long before, which no one had thought of avenging in this drastic fashion. While refusing to believe that the Marranos of this place were actually in danger, he alleged that persons in this category had only themselves to blame if on their escape from Portugal they continued to live under fickle Christian rule, with the sword hanging continuously over their heads, instead of coming to enjoy safety under the sultan's tolerant sway; indeed, he felt inclined to punish by a ban of excommunication this shocking error of judgment rather than mere trading with Ancona. He approved, however, of the suggestion put forward by some well-meaning persons, that the duke of Urbino should be compensated for his disappointment by a gift of 15,000 or 20,000 ducats to be raised among the Turkish Jews by a special tax; a simple thing, it may be said, for an impecunious rabbi to encourage.

The peering legalism of this document seems strangely

incongruous when a question of such palpitating imme-
diacy was involved. Nevertheless, it was approved (the
author claimed) by a number of the local scholars to
whom he read it, though only two — Moses ibn Jamal
and Moses de Segovia — dared the resentment of the
House of Nasi and actually subscribed to it with him.
At the same time, Rabbi Soncino drew up a long and
highly-colored account of the circumstances and his own
impeccable attitude throughout, which he circulated to
the Jewish communities all over the Levant, confident
that, away from Constantinople, scholars would be able
to judge the matter more objectively and to organize
opposition to the attempt that he considered so iniquitous.
The views of a scholar so eminent and so disinterested
could not fail to carry weight.[21]

In a last effort, Doña Gracia had meanwhile written to
the rabbis of all the great communities of the empire,
imploring them to recall the precarious lot of their coreligionists in Pesaro, who would be sacrificed to their duke's
vengeance if the agreement made with him were not
carried out. The well-being of Jews, she reminded them
despairingly, should weigh with their brethren in faith
far above any material interest. Among the opinions
which she received in favor of the boycott, and in opposition to Soncino's views, were those of two of the most
eminent rabbis of the age — Joseph Caro, the author of
the famous code of Jewish religious law, the *Shulhan
Arukh*, and his son-in-law, Moses ben Jacob di Trani
("Mitrani"), pillars of the great mysticals chool at Safed.
The latter, in a closely argued but hardly vigorous document, refuted Soncino on his own ground; he expressed
his confidence, moreover, that the Pesaro merchants

would make good any financial loss that might be incurred by those of Turkey through the use of that port, and pointed out how Doña Gracia had herself taken the lead in the course that she was now advocating.

The weight of learning was not unevenly distributed. But a blockade, to be legal, must be complete; and a boycott, to be effective, must be universal. There was sufficient support for those who opposed the ban, and sufficient erudition displayed on their behalf, for them to brave it with complete impunity, and once they did so others could not afford to hold out. This marked the end of the attempt. The trade of the port of Ancona slowly began to revive. It was not long before a Levantine synagogue frequented by the merchants from the Turkish empire again flourished there, as it continued to do for centuries. The *Señora* had been defeated by the rabbi. But of one thing we may be certain: whoever drew back, Doña Gracia did not; and it is highly improbable that any cargo destined for or despatched by the firm of Nasi ever again passed through the greatest port of the Papal States.

As for the Marranos of Pesaro, they were left to their fate. Doña Gracia and her supporters had their judgment amply confirmed by events; and Soncino, notwithstanding his profound talmudic learning, was proved to be a poor judge of current affairs. He had considered the matter from the quiet of his study, in accordance with his researches into Jewish law; his opponents at the Nasi mansion in Galata knew the circumstances of European politics and the mentality of European politicians. As they anticipated, the duke of Urbino considered himself sorely deceived and injured. Smarting under the disappointment, he had neither the fortitude nor the inclination to resist any longer the pressure brought upon him by the Pope. Moreover, he was in negotiations with the emperor with a view to being appointed captain general of the Spanish troops in Italy, and this too must have influenced him. In March, 1558, he issued an edict banishing the Marranos from his dominions — not only those who had arrived from Ancona, but also the handful already settled there before. It says much for his tolerance that he did not hand them over to ecclesiastical vengeance. The physician Amatus Lusitanus now had to go into exile once again, settling first in the independent republic of Ragusa on the Balkan coast, and then, afraid of further reliance on Christian mercies, at Salonica, where his association with the House of Nasi was renewed. But not all were so fortunate. The mariners of Ancona, jubilant at their triumph, considered the infidel fugitives fair prey wherever they might be found. One ship was chased by them as far as the Istrian peninsula, only the humanity of the captain saving those on board from capture and enslavement. Another vessel, after landing some passengers at Ragusa (perhaps Amatus was one of them), was betrayed to the pirates by the captain himself, who sold the remainder — upwards of fifty souls — into slavery in Apulia.

Even now the Pope was not placated. Some of the Marrano refugees from Ancona had settled in Ferrara where, on Christmas Day of 1555, Duke Ercole guaranteed them the same privileges that they had received from Popes Paul III and Julius III. Pressure was now brought on him to follow the duke of Urbino's example and, on June 9, 1558, the Inquisitor General of the

Roman Inquisition, Cardinal Michael Ghislieri (later Pope, as Pius V), wrote to him demanding that he should likewise send away from his dominions "the perfidious and abominable race of Marranos, unworthy of the consort of human beings, much less of Christians." The duke had too lively an appreciation of the economic importance of the refugees to consent to this (though a quarter of a century later his son proved more compliant). Nevertheless it was impossible for him to withstand the pressure brought upon him to ferret out and destroy all the copies of Jacob da Fano's elegy on the martyrs of Ancona and to punish both author and printer,[22] so that the press maintained by Doña Gracia's protégé, Abraham Usque, was now closed. As for the Jews in the States of the Church, the withdrawal of the boycott did not lighten their lot, and they had to endure more and more suffering until the Pope's death in 1559, greeted with relief and enthusiasm by his subjects as a whole.

For Doña Gracia it was a distressing check — perhaps the most distressing of her career. That her coreligionists would not obey her was bad enough; that she was thwarted by one from whom she anticipated subservience was worse (though she does not seem to have harbored rancor because of this). But worst of all was the defeat. For once the Jews had it in their power to avenge a wrong; but they had not taken their opportunity. Ancona was unpunished, the duke of Urbino unrewarded, the Pope given no reason to repent for his policy of persecution. Jewish solidarity was shown in the eyes of all the world to be a figment, and political action by Jews to improve their position to be utterly ludicrous. The generations that followed were to witness unending persecution and agony for the Jews in the Papal States, and in Christian Europe as a whole. Never again, almost until our own day, was concerted political or economic action attempted by their coreligionists on their behalf. Had the attempt of 1556/7 been successful, it would certainly have been the forerunner of others. Perhaps much suffering might have been prevented; at the worst, there would have been the satisfaction of escaping from the eternal soul-numbing inactivity. Doña Gracia Nasi had at least done all that she could. It is amazing that it was a woman who had taken the lead in this gallant demonstration that it was not always necessary for Jews to suffer injury passively.

ADDITIONAL NOTE TO CHAPTER VII

A DOCUMENT ON THE ANCONA BOYCOTT

As a specimen of the polemic on the subject of the Ancona boycott, and of the correspondence of the rabbis on the subject, the following excerpt is given from the responsa of Joshua Soncino, *Nahala li-Jehoshua* (Constantinople, 1731), § xxxix:—

QUESTION: A messenger has come here, despatched from the city of Pesaro, the place where the fugitives from Ancona have taken refuge. He has informed us of all the good which the duke of Urbino so abundantly wrought at the time of the woes which befell our brethren, who were burned alive [at Ancona] for the sanctification of the Blessed Name of God. On behalf of these fugitives, he requests that an agreement be made, in all the dispersal of Israel, not to do any trade with Ancona, so that any person who normally travels thither for business should go instead to Pesaro, a city of the duke of Urbino. From this, two consequences will result. In the first place, Ancona will not escape vengeance for the blood of our brethren that was shed in that city; and in the second, the rest of the remnant will be permitted to abide in quiet, when the duke perceives the many advantages that will result from the establishment of commerce in his territory. On the other hand, if this agreement is not made, it is almost certain that the duke will be enraged, and that he will uproot all the Jews who are living in his dominions; for he has already heard something of this plan, and indeed received them in the first place upon this understanding. . . .

When the Jews of Ancona heard that those of Pesaro had sent to make this request, they wrote letters to all parts, saying that such an agreement would be as thorns and nettles for all the Jews who live under the Pope's rule; for his anger would be kindled, and his wrath would go forth as fire, all Israel being sureties the one for the other. Accordingly, he would destroy all the Jews who are living in his dominions, saying: "Your brethren who dwell in Turkey are vexing me only because I am zealous for my Faith". . . .

CHAPTER VIII

Journey's End

THE family circle in Constantinople had now for a long time been complete. Doña Gracia's nephew, Joseph, Duke of Naxos after 1566, had for some years been playing a more and more prominent part in Turkish and even international politics, as will be described in due course, in the sequel to the present account. His wife, Reyna, Doña Gracia's adored daughter, was with him, following her mother's example on a smaller scale and engaged in unobtrusive acts of benevolence. Of the elder Reyna, Gracia's sister and widow of the Antwerp merchant-prince Diogo Mendes, her brother-in-law, little more is heard after her escape from Venice subsequent to her momentary aberration; she had been expected to come with the rest of the family to Turkey, but had been kept back as it seems for some unknown reason, at least for a time.[1] Without doubt, she followed the rest, being in the Levant as it seems at the time of the lawsuit about the division of the family property in 1554–5. However that may be, she had by now ceased to play anything of a public role, and one may perhaps imagine her disconsolate existence in the Nasi mansion, pining after the Court life of Brussels, the pageants of Venice, the brilliant society of Ferrara.[1] In any case, it does not appear that she survived for long.

Her daughter, on the other hand, Gracia *la chica*, with her husband, Samuel Nasi (Don Joseph's brother), had not been without their excitements in the meanwhile. When the rest of the family left Italy, the latter had apparently been left behind to look after the business interests of the firm (unless perhaps he had returned thither later on). In any case, at the time of the onslaught against the Marranos of Ancona in 1555, the couple were living in Ferrara, or else took refuge there. The danger of their situation was manifest. Doña Gracia's local agents, Agostino Enriques and Duarte Gomez, were now denounced to the local tribunal of the Holy Office. Though no positive evidence of religious backsliding could be produced against them and the charges were dismissed, this episode showed how precarious the position of the New Christian element was even at this coveted haven of refuge. Members of the notorious House of Mendes, who personified the Marrano to the outside world, obviously ran exceptional risks. Doña Gracia was profoundly alarmed therefore at the possibility of a prosecution of her niece and nephew on the score of apostasy, which at the best might cost them all their property, at the worst, their lives.

But just as the diplomacy of the Sublime Porte had been exerted not so long before to safeguard her, so she was now able to have the same machinery set in motion on behalf of others, thanks to her excellent relations with the grand vizier, Rustam Pasha. Early in 1556, the populace of Ferrara was deeply stirred and impressed by the arrival of an envoy named Hassan from the sultan's son and co-ruler, Selim, and by the gifts which he received from the duke — two robes in the Turkish style, including a tunic in gold brocade, together with a purse of 400 ducats in cash. He remained in the city from February 1 to March 3, returning again after a short absence on March 19 and remaining for four days; and when he passed through Ragusa on his return journey on May 4, the government of that republic gave him a gratuity of twenty zecchins. The reason for the mission of this highly honored diplomat was, it transpired, to request the duke to despatch Doña Gracia's nephew safe and sound to Constantinople together with his wife, property and household.[2]

Strong influences were, however, brought to bear in the other direction, presumably by the emperor and the Pope; for, notwithstanding this strongly-supported request, the duke refused to grant the necessary safe-conduct. Don Samuel and his household had to remain therefore in Ferrara, perhaps unmolested, but knowing that their lives depended upon the good will and good health of the elderly duke, whose successor was less certain to be so tolerant.

The part taken by the House of Nasi in organizing the Ancona boycott made the danger all the more imminent, but nevertheless nothing could be done. Negotiations and communications were protracted for two years. Doña Gracia continued to exert what influence she had at the Sublime Porte in favor of her kinsfolk. The sultan and the grand vizier despatched missive after missive to Ferrara. Duke Ercole asked for a passport for an ambassador he wished to send to Constantinople to discuss the matter but, although this was duly received, we do not know of any sequel. Meanwhile, yet another denunciation of Duarte Gomez and Agostino Enriques before the

Holy Office at Venice, in September, 1557, though it led
to no result, emphasized the potential danger to Marranos anywhere in Italy, even as regards persons who
had not declared their Judaism. At last, on March 6,
1558, the duke of Ferrara informed Rustam Pasha that
he had no objection to the departure of "the Jew, brother
of Zuan Miches" [i. e., João Miguez] — only just in time,
for almost immediately after this the Grand Inquisitor,
Cardinal Ghislieri, began to exert pressure on him to take
drastic proceedings against the Marranos in his dominions.[3] Now at last, Don Samuel and his wife rejoined
their kinsfolk in Constantinople, and the family circle
was re-united.

Doña Gracia's interests in Ferrara were not, indeed,
wound up, though her relations there with her husband's
kinsman, Agostino Enriques, whom she had left in
charge, proved a grievous disappointment. He had long
refrained — no doubt to her great distress — from following her example in embracing Judaism. He owed a
good deal of money to her Florentine correspondent,
Luca degli Albizzi, as a result of which the latter refused
to transmit to her the very considerable sums he held on
her account. When the troubles started for the Jews and
Marranos in Italy in 1555, and she asked him as a pre-
cautionary measure to transfer her funds back to her
name, he demurred. He failed to answer her letters; he
refused to treat with Samuel de Ardeiro, the agent she
sent to take charge of her interests in 1558, on the grounds
that he did not trust him sufficiently; he would not
answer a summons to justify himself before the duke
of Ferrara, because (as he ingeniously explained) his safe-
conduct absolved him from being prosecuted in that city

except by natives. When at last he condescended to
put forward a justification of his actions, he alleged that
he had laid out a great deal of money on behalf of Gracia
la chica, perhaps in connection with the recent negotiations for her and her husband's release — an expenditure,
the older lady pointed out indignantly, which the other
could perfectly well afford alone, without assistance from
anyone else. As for herself, she added, she always paid
her debts, but she had been told nothing before of this
claim. Even a personal letter of April, 1559, filled with
magnificent indignation, which was delivered to him by
his associate, Duarte Gomez (with whom he was told
that he might negotiate), had no tangible result. (We
are indebted to this episode, incidentally, for the solitary
extant specimen of Doña Gracia's epistolary style, unfortunately too long and complicated to be quoted here at
length.) When in the end her patience was exhausted,
and she obtained Turkish diplomatic intervention to
secure judgment (her usual expedient, used so often),
this man, who had so long and so persistently refused to
return to the faith of his fathers, declared himself a Jew,
under the name of Abraham Benveniste, and asked the
local rabbis to adjudicate the case in accordance with
talmudic law, which he imagined would in these special
circumstances be more favorable to him. Gracia might,
of course, have refused outright to submit to such juris-
diction. Nevertheless, "in her great Jewishness and
righteousness" (as one of her admirers phrased it), she
preferred to have a definite ruling from the rabbis on the
question as to whether in a case such as this, where she
was dealing with a person who had carried on all his
transactions with her hitherto as a Christian, and obvi-

ously took this course only as a subterfuge, she was legally
and morally obliged to argue the matter out before a
Jewish tribunal and in accordance with Jewish law. The
problem was referred (apparently in 1562) to Rabbi
Joshua Soncino. He, notwithstanding his relentless opposition to her in the matter of the Ancona boycott not so
long before, decided that she was completely justified in
the course she had taken and that no blame should be
attached to her if she secured a verdict from the secular
judges. The decision at which they arrived is not on
record. It is nevertheless probable that she was successful and obtained a favorable verdict, though the recovery
of her capital would have been a more difficult task.
Once again, the support she received from the Turkish
authorities was noteworthy.[4]

Her active life, eventful to the last, was by now drawing to its close. It was perhaps part of Doña Gracia's
matriarchal role that she was something of a valetudinarian. In her prime, we saw her excusing herself from
an unpleasant interview with the queen regent of the
Netherlands on the ground of illness, and later on, Amatus
Lusitanus, her physician, hints at her preoccupation with
her health. Indeed, the family record of barren marriages
and only children and early deaths seems to suggest a
somewhat unhealthy stock. Her disturbed, anxious, zest-
ful career is unlikely to have fortified her constitution,
nor was life in the sultry, overcrowded, insanitary Constantinople of four centuries ago calculated to favor lon-
gevity. From the beginning of the fifteen-sixties, less
and less is heard of her, more and more of her illustrious
nephew and son-in-law. Clearly, she had now withdrawn
to some extent into retirement.

She herself, pious Jewess that she was, had long intended to end her days in the Holy Land, so as to be laid at the last by her husband's side in the Valley of Jehoshaphat. She even had a mansion prepared at Tiberias as her residence, and obtained from the sultan special privileges with the object of creating a new and self-dependent Jewish settlement there paying, it was said, 1,000 ducats yearly for the concession.[5] In 1565, a Portuguese visitor found that the Jewish inhabitants of the Holy Land were all excited at the prospect of the immediate arrival of the *Señora*, as she was generally called even here. But, like lesser humanity, she apparently delayed the grand climacteric too long, so that at the last she was not vouchsafed even a Pisgah-sight of the land of her mystical dreams and ideals.[6]

Precisely when and where her death took place is unknown. Turkish records of the period are fragmentary, while the muniments of the Jewish communities of the Near East are in a hopelessly inadequate state, so that we receive from them no guidance on matters of this sort. However, her death is referred to, apparently as something recent, in the early summer of 1569,[7] and it probably did not take place long before. She was by no means old — probably not beyond her sixtieth year, though that was considered a ripe age in those days. She had survived her husband by a full quarter of a century or more, crowded with episode, adventure and good deeds.

The news of the *Señora's* death was received throughout the Jewish world with a sense of profoundest grief. Everywhere memorial services were held, such as were seldom

SULEIMAN THE MAGNIFICENT
from a drawing in the Museo Correr

TITLE PAGE OF SAADIA LUNGO'S BOOK
Sefer Seder Zemanim

known among Jews at that time except on the occasion
of the death of rabbis of profoundest learning. Moses
Almosnino, who officiated in the synagogue she had
founded in Salonica, commemorated her there in an eloquent address, and again a month later in Adrianople,
when the traditional thirty days of deep formal mourn-
ing were ended.[8] It is not to be doubted that her memory
was similarly honored in other congregations of the Ottoman empire and far beyond it. Saadiah Lungo, poet-in-
ordinary of the Salonica community, who kept the spark
of the Hispano-Jewish school of singers alive in a remote
land, celebrated her in a lengthy but inchoate elegy —
the only one in all his works dedicated to a woman — in
which he placed her life's work in the setting of Marrano
activity and tribulation: —

> Of all we treasured most we stand bereft
> > Throughout the lands of thy dispersal, Ariel;
> > And every mother-town in Israel
> Weeps for the fate of those in anguish left.
> > > Gone is the glitter;
> > > My mourning is bitter,
> > > And broken my heart.

"All good qualities were joined in her," he summed up,
with no element of exaggeration or insincerity; and his
sentiments were generally shared.

And not among the communal leaders alone. There
was grief among the paupers whom she had fed at her
table, among the scholars whom she had sustained,
among the ordinary men and women who looked up to
her as their representative and benefactress; grief in
Tiberias, where she had hoped to live, and elsewhere in

the Holy Land, where her benevolence had been so un-
stinted; grief in Ferrara, where so many of those whom
she had helped to escape from certain martyrdom were
still residing; grief in Flanders, where the memory of her
courage and endeavors was still fresh; grief, above all,
among the Marranos of Portugal, now deprived of their
greatest support and the firmest hope in their distress.
Never perhaps in the whole of Jewish history, since the
days of Salome Alexandra, the Hasmonean queen of
Judea sixteen hundred years before, had a woman's
death been so generally and so profoundly mourned.
Nor, down to our own day, has any other Jewish woman
attained quite the same outstanding position — not even
Judith Montefiore, Sir Moses Montefiore's inspiration
and support; nor even perhaps Henrietta Szold, who in
our time devoted herself to the task of saving children
from the hell of Central Europe with the same spirit of
devotion that Gracia Nasi applied in the sixteenth century to the salvation of the Marranos from Portugal.

Her example did not die. Those who read the works
dedicated to her could not fail to be impressed by her
personality, shining through the stilted verbiage of
Renaissance rhetoric. Moreover, in their great palace
overlooking the Bosphorus, her example was long maintained by her daughter and companion in so many
adventures, Doña Reyna, and her son-in-law, the former
João Miguez, now Duke of Naxos, whose career outdid
even hers for sheer romance, though not for nobility.

That is another story, which must await another opportunity for telling.

CHRONOLOGICAL TABLE

BIBLIOGRAPHY

BIBLIOGRAPHY

I mention here generally only the works specifically dealing with the career of Gracia Nasi and her nephew: they have sometimes been used in other chapters besides those in connection with which they are set down. I have given exact references in the text, to assist the student, only for statements which cannot be readily verified from these works. I am not listing the very numerous popular and semi-popular articles written on this attractive subject.

I. GENERAL

BATO, YOM-TOB (LUDWIG), Don Joseph Nasi (a romanticized biography, in Hebrew). Tel-Aviv, 1942.

CARMOLY, E., Don Josef, Duc de Naxos. Brussels, 1855.

CHASSAZOGLU, N., Josef Nasi, der jüdische Prinz der griechischen Iseln.

GALANTE, ABRAHAM, Don Joseph Nassi, Duc de Naxos, d'après des nouveaux documents. Constantinople, 1913.

GRAETZ, H., Geschichte der Juden, vol. IX.

———, Don Joseph, Herzog von Naxos, Graf von Andros, und Donna Gracia Nassi, in *Jahrbuch für Israeliten*, ed. Wertheimer. Vienna, 1856.

HALPHEN, ALICE FERNAND, Une grande dame Juive de la Renaissance: Gracia Mendesia-Nasi. Paris, 1929.

LEVY, M. A., Don Joseph Nasi, Herzog von Naxos, seine Familie, und zwei jüdische Diplomaten seiner Zeit. Breslau, 1859.

REZNIK, J., Le Duc Joseph de Naxos: contribution à l'histoire juive du XVIe siècle. Paris, 1936.

WILDENRAT, JOHANN VON, Joseph Nasi (a novel) (translated into Hebrew by P. Kaplan). Warsaw, 1899.

CHAPTER I

The House of Mendes

D'AZEVEDO, J. LUCIO, Historia dos Christãos Novos Portugueses. Lisbon, 1921.

REMEDIOS, J. MENDES DOS, Os Judeus em Portugal, 2 vols. Lisbon, 1895–1928.

ROTH, C., History of the Marranos (revised ed.). Philadelphia, 1941.

CHAPTER II

Antwerp

GINSBURGER, E., Marie de Hongrie, Charles-Quint, les veuves Mendès, et les néo-Chrétiens, in *Revue des Etudes Juives*, LXXXIX, 179–192.
GORIS, J. A., Les colonies marchandes méridionales à Anvers. Louvain, 1925.
LEMOS, M., Amatus Lusitanus. Porto, 1914.
LOPES, J. M., Les Portugais à Anvers. Antwerp, 1895.
ULLMANN, S., Histoire des Juifs en Belgique jusqu'au 18e siècle. Antwerp, n. d.
———, Studien zur Geschichte der Juden in Belgien. Antwerp, 1909.
WEGG, JERVIS, Antwerp, 1477–1559. London, 1916.

CHAPTER III

Venice

ROTH, C., History of the Jews in Venice. Philadelphia, 1930.
———, Les Marranes à Venise, in *Revue des Etudes Juives*, LXXXIX, 201–223.

CHAPTER IV

Ferrara

BALLETTI, A., Gli ebrei e gli estensi. 2nd ed., Reggio, 1930.
ROTH, C., Salusque Lusitano, in *Jewish Quarterly Review*, N. S., XXXIV, 65–85.
———, The Marrano Press at Ferrara, 1552–1555, in *Modern Language Review*, XXXVIII, 307–317.
USQUE, SAMUEL, Consolaçam ás Tribulaçoens de Israel, ed. Mendes dos Remedios. Coimbra, 1906.

CHAPTER V

Constantinople

FRANCO, M., Essai sur l'Histoire des Israélites de l'Empire Ottoman depuis les origines jusqu' à nos jours. Paris, 1897.

GALANTE, ABRAHAM, Histoire des Juifs d'Istanbul. 2 vols. Constantinople, 1942.

———, Deux nouveaux documents sur Doña Gracia Nassy, in *Revue des Etudes Juives*, LXV, 151–54.

HAMMER-PURGSTALL, J. VON, Geschichte des Osmanischen Reichte (esp. volumes ii and iii). French edition trs. J. J. Helbert. Paris, 1835–43.

JORGA, N., Geschichte des Osmanischen Reiches, 5 vols. (esp. vol. III). Gotha, 1913.

MERRIMAN, R. B., Suleiman the Magnificent. Cambridge, Mass., 1944.

ROSANES, S. A., Divre Yeme Israel be-Togarma (History of the Jews in Turkey), vol. II. 2nd ed., Sofia, 1938.

ZINKEISEN, J. W., Geschichte des Osmanischen Reiches in Europa (esp. volume II). Hamburg and Gotha, 1840–63.

CHAPTER VI

"The Heart of Her People"

EMMANUEL, I. S., Histoire des Israélites de Salonique, vol. I (all published). Paris, 1936.

GALANTE, A., Les Synagogues d'Istanbul. Constantinople, 1937.

CHAPTER VII

The Ancona Boycott

BERNFELD, S., Sepher ha-Demaoth (Hebrew), II, 320–350.

FERROSO (MARONI) C., Di alcuni ebrei portoghesi giustiziati in Ancona sotto Paolo IV, in *Archivio storico Marche e Umbria*, I, 689–719.

GARIBALDI, G., Un asserto Autodafé sotto Paolo IV. Bologna, 1876.

GRUNEBAUM, P., Un episode de l'histoire des Juifs d'Ancône, in *Revue des Etudes Juives*, XXVIII, 142–6.

Kaufmann, D., Les martyrs d'Ancône, in *Revue des Etudes Juives*, XI, 149–153.

———, Les marranes de Pesaro et les represailles des juifs levantins contre la ville d'Ancône, *ibid.*, XVI, 61–72.

———, Deux lettres nouvelles des Marranes de Pesaro touchant l'interruption des affaires avec Ancône, *ibid.*, XXXI, 231–9.

———, La quête pour les marranes expulsés de Pesaro, *ibid.*, XX, 47–8.

———, Les 24 martyrs d'Ancône, *ibid.*, XXXI, 222–230.

Responsa (Hebrew) of Joshua Soncino, XXXIX, XL; of Joseph ibn Leb, I, 63b–64a; of Moses di Trani, I, 237: of Samuel di Medina, IV, 59.

Rosenberg, H., Elégie de Mordekhai ben Yehouda di Blanes sur les 24 martyrs d'Ancône, *Revue des Etudes Juives*, XC, 166–8.

Sonne, I., Une source nouvelle pour l'histoire des martyrs d'Ancône, *ibid.*, LXXXIX, 360–380.

NOTES

NOTES

Notes to Chapter I

[1] The majority of the Portuguese Jews at the time of the final tragedy were of Spanish origin, and the names of the families with which this book is principally concerned imply the same extraction. For the general story, see my *History of the Marranos* (2nd edition, Philadelphia, 1941).

[2] There are full details of the forced conversion in Portugal and the succeeding events in my *History of the Marranos*; in these pages it is necessary to give only a brief recapitulation.

[3] See Additional Note at the end of this chapter for a discussion of this complicated and confused problem of genealogy and nomenclature.

[4] These names are given in the safe-conduct published by Balletti, *Gli ebrei e gli estensi* (see below, page 63). It is probable that the two brothers, who died in 1536 and 1542/3 respectively and had already been active for many years, must have been born before the banishment of the Jews from Spain. But the details given in the text are put forward only tentatively and hesitantly.

[5] Balletti, *loc. cit.* It is, of course, out of the question that this Henrique Nuñez was identical with the notorious informer against the Marranos of the same name, known as *Firme Fé*, who ultimately met his fate at the hands of his victims (Roth, *Marranos*, pp. 67-8).

It is a curious coincidence that those editions of Amatus Lusitanus' sixth "century" which were published in Italy bear a dedication to "Dr. Henrico Nuñes" instead of to Don Joseph Nasi (see below, page 138, and my approaching volume on the Duke of Naxos): he may have been a member of the family, but I am unable to suggest a connection.

[6] See Hans Dernschwam's *Diary*, quoted below, page 84. This is, however, the only source which gives the name or profession of the Duke of Naxos' father (I think that Lucien Wolf, *Essays in Jewish History*, p. 76, was relying on this, and not on an Inquisitional source), and I repeat the statement with due reserve. See for the whole question the Additional Note at the end of this chapter.

[7] I have not, of course, exhausted the list: there was, for example, also a *Nasi* Shealtiel, whose son died as the result of the collapse of a house at Monza de Campos in 1097, and a *Nasi* Abraham, whose son Judah lived at Leon before 1094, to mention only two out of many.

[8] F. Baer, *Die Juden im christlichen Spanien*, II. 347.

⁹ The dedication to the Ferrara Bible of 1553 (below, p. 74) seems to suggest that her native country (*patria*) was Spain, which is likely enough; but I do not think that the geographical and political borderline between Spain and Portugal would have been taken too seriously in a rhetorical effusion of this sort.

¹⁰ Both niece and aunt bore the same name subsequently, as Jewesses; it is likely enough that the same had been the case earlier.

¹¹ L. Wolf, *Essays in Jewish History*, p. 76. Unfortunately, I have not been able to trace among the author's papers the document (I believe from the Flemish archives) on which this statement was based.

Notes to Chapter II

¹ There was a close parallel to this, of course, twenty-five centuries before when, by building a fleet on the Red Sea, King Solomon similarly exploited the sea-route to India: "And King Solomon made a navy of ships in Eziongeber, which is beside Eloth... and they came to Ophir and fetched thence gold... and brought it to king Solomon... and the queen of Sheba... gave the king an hundred and twenty talents of gold and of spices very great store, and precious stones: there came no more such abundance of spices as these ...." (I Kings, 9.26–10.10).

² Details of Diogo Mendes' life in Antwerp may be reconstructed from two curiously different categories of source material — on the one hand, the responsa of Joshua Soncino, § xx, and those of other rabbis of the period who were later on consulted about the administration of his estate (see below, pages 108–111); and, on the other, the various works on sixteenth-century Antwerp, listed in the bibliography to this chapter. He figures in these very prominently indeed, and it would be wearisome to collect all the data.

³ See for this Richard Ehrenberg's book, *Capital and Finance in the Age of the Renaissance*.

⁴ The equivalent in modern values would be something like £1,000,000 sterling, or $5,000,000.

⁵ A Juan Rodrigues was prosecuted in 1534 for being in the country without permission (Goris, *Les colonies marchandes méridionales à Anvers*, p. 651), but it is hardly likely that this can be the same man.

⁶ Amatus Lusitanus, *Dioscorides*, I. 120.

⁷ Like Amatus Lusitanus, he will also figure frequently later on in this story: see pages 138 ff.

⁸ In one or two contemporary sources (see for example the report of 1564 on the New Christians, cited below, page 120), the name of the wealthy Marrano woman who settled in Turkey as a Jewess is given as "Madonna Brianda," which form figures also in the Ferrara safe-

conduct of 1550. Since so far as we know Gracia Nasi was never so called, I conclude (though not dogmatically) that it applied to her sister.

[9] I. Prins, *De Vestiging der Marranen in Noord Nederland*, p. 40 n., speaks of a son of Diego Mendes named Antonio Martinez, which would imply an earlier marriage (not, certainly, improbable); but reference to the sources makes it clear that this is based on a confusion. Before the marriage it had been understood that, if he remained childless, Diogo would adopt his brother's child as his own.

[10] This was the conclusion of the rabbis consulted later on about the disposal of the estate: see below, pages 108–111.

[11] This amazing story was first told by Lucien Wolf, *Essays in Jewish History*, p. 76 ff.

[12] Goris, *Les colonies marchandes méridionales à Anvers*, p. 566.

[13] A. Herculano, *Historia do origem e estabelicimento da Inquisicão em Portugal*, book IV.

[14] Wolf, *Essays*, p. 76.

[15] Wolf, *Essays*, pp. 81–2. It is to be hoped that the documents on which this memorable story is based will soon be published.

[16] This account differs from that which I have given elsewhere, basing myself on the details given by Wolf in his *Essays*, p. 83, which I now find to be misleading.

[17] Goris, *Les colonies marchandes méridionales à Anvers*, p. 651, states that he was accused and fled in this year, his goods being confiscated. But this inference, not based on any definite record, cannot be reconciled with the information given elsewhere. On the other hand, it seems that he thought it best to lie low for a time, as his name disappears from the records after June, 1540 (*Ibid.*, p. 575; the Diogo Mendez of 1553, however, is another person).

[18] Goris, p. 272.

[19] J. M. Lopes in *Les Portugais à Anvers*, gives part of the text of Diogo Mendes' will, from the original Ms. in the local archives, in French. A further portion is preserved, most astonishingly, in Spanish (in Hebrew characters) in the responsa of Moses di Trani, § lxxx.

[20] *Letters and Papers, Henry VIII*, xix. 513 ff.

[21] This detail, absent from the Flemish records published thus far, is provided in the responsa of Rabbis Moses di Trani and Joshua Soncino (see below, pages 108–111). It is borne out, however, by a casual reference in the other sources (see below, page 110) — a curious example of historical dovetailing.

[22] J. Lucio d'Azevedo, *Historia dos christãos novos Portugueses*, p. 368: the damsel is referred to as being the daughter of Francisco Mendes Bemvisto (=Benveniste), demonstrating how notorious the Jewish origin of the family must have been.

²³ Verbal communication on more than one occasion from the late Lucien Wolf, based on a record which I have been unable to trace among his papers.

²⁴ It is generally stated that the family left Antwerp in 1543. But from the documents published by Ginsburger in the *Revue des Etudes Juives*, LXXXIX, 179–192, it is obvious that they were still in Flanders in May, 1544, and had fled some while before April, 1545. From the Hebrew sources, it appears that the flight took place some two years after Diogo Mendes' death, i. e., in the winter of 1544–5.

²⁵ This point will be discussed more fully in the second part of this work, *The Duke of Naxos*.

²⁶ The reader who wants full details of this may find them in an article by E. Ginsburger in the *Revue des Etudes Juives*, LXXXIX, 179–192 (see bibliography to this chapter); it would be wearisome and pointless to repeat them here in all their trivialities.

Notes to Chapter III

¹ For the general background of the Jewish scene here, see my *History of the Jews in Venice* (Philadelphia, 1930) and, on a broader canvas, my recent *History of the Jews in Italy* (Philadelphia, 1946).

² Amatus Lusitanus, *Dioscorides*, I. 120.

³ There is, however, occasional confusion on this point, as we have seen, Doña Beatrice herself being sometimes called by this name.

⁴ This is the same word, originally meaning "bow-maker," which was rendered in English in the nineteenth century as *kavass*; but it would be an anachronism to use this form here.

⁵ ="Bailiff": virtually, consular agent and magistrate.

⁶ This would imply December, 1548, or January, 1549; but it may only have been for a visit. The definite transference seems to have taken place a little later.

⁷ See below, page 73 for this interesting personality.

⁸ Balletti, *Gli ebrei e gli estensi*, 2nd ed., pp. 77–8. It can hardly be doubted that this document refers to the Nasi sisters — the coincidence of the names *Reyna* and *Benveniste* seems decisive — but there are some obvious inconsistencies in the descriptions. "Vellida" (?=(Ben)venida) must necessarily correspond here to Gracia: the same name was borne by the wife of Don Joseph Abrabanel (d. 1616).

⁹ I have become less certain about this since writing these lines. There is a possibility that the name of Nasi was not adopted before reaching Constantinople (as, in fact, one contemporary observer stated: below, page 84). The books dedicated to her at Ferrara under the name Doña Gracia Nasi (see below) were not, in fact, published

until after she left that city, even though prepared before: and the medal bearing this name does not seem to be anterior to the year 1555, as will be shown.

Notes to Chapter IV

[1] This detail (Balletti, *Gli ebrei e gli estensi*, p. 77) is an interesting addition to our very sparse knowledge of the hunting-down of the Marranos in this year.

[2] I can find no contemporary authority for this frequently-repeated statement, which I set down only with the utmost reserve. I have the impression that it is one of the "many inventions" of Eliakim Carmoly, who was at the same time one of the most industrious and one of the least reliable of the Jewish savants of the last century.

[3] In view of the fact that sons-in-law are mentioned in the safe-conduct of 1550, which has been spoken of above, it is possible that the marriage took place before leaving Venice. But these additions to the family may have been mentioned in intelligent anticipation only. I imagine that the famous medal of Gracia Nasi, described below p. 73, was struck on the occasion of her marriage, which would thus have taken place when she was eighteen years of age.

Samuel Nasi was known later on by the alternative name Moses; but this, apparently applied at the time of illness, cannot have been his Marrano appellation.

[4] In his pharmaceutical work, *Dioscorides*, IV, 171.

[5] It hardly need be stated that Italy was the classical land of the quasi-emancipation of the Jewish women in former days. There is even said to have been, in the fourteenth century, a Jewish poetess, Giustina Levi Perotti, who exchanged sonnets with Petrarch. She may be a figment of Renaissance imagination. But a little after Doña Gracia's day two literary figures made their mark — the poetess Deborah Ascarelli in Rome and Sarah Coppio Sullam, who maintained a literary salon in the Ghetto of Venice.

Several Jewish women in Italy in the period with which we are dealing were proficient in the incongruous but difficult art of *Shehita*, or ritual slaughter, which required a considerable degree of scholarship: some of their licenses are extant.

[6] He has hitherto been identified with the poet Salomon Usque (or Salusque Lusitano), who also translated Petrarch: see for him below, pp. 118 and 119. But this identification is based on a misunderstanding: see my article in *Jewish Quarterly Review*, N. S. XXXIV, 65–85, where the confusion is I hope cleared up.

[7] The work has also been ascribed by some experts to another eminent engraver-artist, Giovanni Paolo Poggini.

[8] The legend on the medal makes it quite clear that it does not represent the elder Gracia, as has so often been stated, unless the artist executed it from a painting made many years before, which would have been pointless as well as unusual, and indeed hardly flattering. From the fact that the subject is called "Nasi," not "Benveniste," it must be assumed that she was already married to her cousin: indeed, as suggested above, the medal was perhaps struck in honor of the wedding. Since her parents are said to have married in or after 1536, she is unlikely to have completed her eighteenth year before 1555, by which time the elder Doña Gracia was already settled in Constantinople.

[9] Perhaps the "Rabbi Yomtob" who acted as Doña Gracia's agent when she began to make arrangements for removal to Ferrara; see above, page 63.

[10] I have described these productions in some detail — and cleared up several long-standing confusions concerning them — in my article, *The Marrano Press in Ferrara*, in the *Modern Language Review*, XXXVIII, 307–317.

It should perhaps be pointed out that Doña Gracia had already left Ferrara by the time that this work, and the one which is considered in the following pages, had appeared; but they were obviously prepared for the press while she was still at hand.

[11] Cf. the deposition of Tomaz Fernandes (1556) in *Miscellanies of the Jewish Historical Society of England*, II. 33–56 — a most interesting human document, quite apart from its historical importance.

[12] To avoid any possibility of misunderstanding, the author here adds a note in the margin: *The Just Doña Gracia Nasci.*

[13] See below, p. 79.

[14] An attentive reading of the text makes it seem probable (the point has, I think, never been noted before) that the work contains a a good deal of autobiographical material, the author's personal experences being treated apparently as typical. It seems pretty certain, for example, that in his own peregrinations he followed the path of exile which he himself depicted with such feeling. Thus he presumably fled from Portugal to England (III.15) where perhaps he arrived in 1531: he mentions indeed (p. 14) the display of traitors' heads on London Bridge as though he had seen it with his own eyes. He then went on by way of Flanders (p. 33) and Germany (pp. 33, 52, 53) and through Switzerland, giving a particularly vivid description of the fugitives' sufferings in the Alpine passes (pp. 33–4). Arrived in Italy, he settled first in Milan (pp. 33, 53) and then in Ferrara, being one of the victims of the expulsion in 1551, of which he speaks with exceptional warmth (p. 37 ff.).

[15] This story, which has never before engaged the attention of his-

torians, is told by Usque, very cryptically, in the *Consolaçam*, III, § 36: he indicates the place only in the Index, where the episode is described as *O desterro de ferr*. (I have verified this from the excessively rare original edition.)

[16] That there was a second visit, followed by a second intervention from Constantinople, is obvious from the despatches published by Charrière, *Negotiations de la France dans le Levant*; it is quite out of the question that the documents of 1551 refer to the same episode as those of 1549, however similar the circumstances may appear.

[17] The episode is recorded by Amatus Lusitanus (*Dioscorides*, II, xxxix) as having taken place while his book was in the press (it was published in 1553): this also suggests a second visit of Doña Gracia's to Venice.

Notes to Chapter V

[1] This remarkable work, *Viaje de Turquia*, contains a great deal of Jewish interest, which thus far has not received much attention. It was originally ascribed by M. Serrano y Sanz, who first published it in his *Autobiografias y Memorias* (Madrid, 1905), to the well-known Spanish litterateur Cristobál de Villalón, but has now been proved by Marcel Bataillon to be the work of Andrés Laguna, the translator of *Dioscorides*. The passage quoted is to be found on p. 251 of the new edition (Buenos Aires, 1942).

[2] From Franz Babinger, *Hans Dernschwam's Tagebuch einer Reise nach Konstantinopel und Kleinasien, 1553-55* (Munich, 1923), p. 106 ff. I have made use, by kind permission, of the English version in J. R. Marcus, *The Jew in the Medieval World* (Cincinnati, 1928), p. 411 ff. For other impressions by this author, see also below, pp. 94-6; and for his impressions of the Jews in general, Porges in *Monatsschrift für die Geschichte und Wissenschaft des Judenthums*, 1924, p. 246 ff.

[3] See Chapter VII, below, *"The Ancona Boycott"*, for a description of this tragic episode.

[4] The details regarding Doña Gracia's relations with the republic of Ragusa, now and later, are taken from the history of that community by Jorjo Tadic, *Jevreji u Dubrovniku*, Sarajevo, 1937.

[5] For Dernschwam's impressions of Doña Gracia, see above, page 84. A few particularly unflattering remarks have been omitted here.

[6] The reference is obviously to Moses Hamon and his son Joseph, concerning whom see above, pp. 56 and 80.

[7] I am making use of the racy eighteenth-century translation in the Harleian Collection (London, 1745).

[8] The reason for this curious form of persecution is that the janissaries had the function of acting as fire-brigade; their perquisite was

anything they found in the houses which they saved or pulled down to prevent the flames from spreading. Incendiarism was thus exceptionally profitable to them.

[8a] Other travellers too speak of the excesses commited against the Jews by these lawless soldiers. Cf. the following description quoted by A. Cohen, *An Anglo-Jewish Scrap-Book* (London 1943), p. 126:

> The Jews are very obnoxious to the insolencies of the Janizaries, who often times to make themselves merry, throw and kick them to the ground and pull them by the noses and by the ears. Against which they dare not so much as open their lips, for fear the sport should by the least ill-word be turned into fury and madness. And very often to do them the more dishonour, when any criminal has received the sentence of death, they presently hurry him away and make the first Jew, rich or poor, they can light upon, walk with the rope in his hand, tied about the neck of the other, till they come to the next tree out of town, and there hang him.

[9] R. Sandys, "A Relation of a Journey Begun in 1610," in *Purchas His Pilgrimes*, VIII, 175. There is a most interesting collection of these passages in A. Cohen's *Anglo-Jewish Scrap-Book*.

[10] Robert Withers, "The Grand Signiors Seraglio," in *Purchas His Pilgrimes*, IX, 346–7.

[11] This, at least, is implied by the historians; but I find it difficult to believe in an activity extending over so long a period. Is it possible that two persons of the same name are in question?

[12] The tragic sequel to the career of Esther Kyra will be told in connection with the biography of Joseph Nasi. In addition to the monograph on her by Abraham Galante (Constantinople, 1926), see the study by J. H. Mordtmann, "Die jüdischen Kira im Serai der Sultane" (*Mitteilungen des Seminars für orientalische Sprachen*, XXXII, ii), where the name is fully discussed.

[13] Translated from the original Italian text published by Ellis, *Original Letters illustrative of English History*, III, 53–5. This document is dated 16th November, 1599. It is conceivable that Esperanza Malchi's influence at the Palace went back to Doña Gracia's day. But in any case she was by no means the only Jewess who performed this sort of service for the sultanas, and the document is thus a typical one.

It may be that Esperanza Malchi was the anonymous Jewish favorite of the sultan's sister who, in 1622, tried to assist Ludovico Locadello to obtain the office of Voivode of Moldavia.

[14] Responsa (*Sheeloth u-Teshuboth*) of Joseph Caro, § § lxxx, lxxxi; (by Moses di Trani): of Samuel de Medina, *Hoshen Mishpat*, § § cccxxvii ff.; of Joshua Soncino, § xii. (For details regarding all these scholars, see below, chapter vii.) The arguments are epitomized in H. Zimmels, *Die Marranen in der rabbinischen Literatur*, pp. 107–113,

and S. Asaf, *Be-Ohole Jaacob*, pp. 172–4. The following ostensible names figure in the correspondence: Gracia Nasi = Hannah; Francisco Mendes = Reuben (the conventional "John Doe" of rabbinical correspondence); Diogo Mendes = Simeon ("Richard Roe"); Reyna (Gracia's daughter) = Sarah; Reyna, widow of Diogo Mendes = Rebecca; Gracia *la chica*, her daughter = Dinah.

I have not gone into all the confusing details of the case, for which recourse may be had to the sources and the works indicated above.

[15] These interesting documents were discovered by Abraham Galante and published by him in the *Revue des Etudes Juives*, LXV, 151–4, and in his *Don Joseph Nasi, Duc de Naxos* (Constantinople, 1913).

[16] For all these data, see Tadic's book on the history of the Jews in Ragusa referred to above, page 201.

[17] This subsequently led to considerable litigation: see the Responsa of Joseph Caro, §§ lxxx (by Moses di Trani) and lxxxi: of Joshua Soncino, § xii; and below, page 179.

For Agostino Henriques and Duarte Gomez see my article "Salusque Lusitano" in the *Jewish Quarterly Review*, N. S., XXXIV, 65–85.

[18] All this will be dealt of in detail in the sequel to this work, *Don Joseph Nasi, Duke of Naxos*; my references to him in this volume will therefore be cursory.

[19] See below, page 173.

[20] See my article, "Salusque Lusitano," in *Jewish Quarterly Review*, N. S., XXXIV, 65–85.

[21] See above, pages 74–5; and for his propaganda in Safed, *Kol Mebaser* by Isaac Akrish (protégé of Esther Kyra and subsequently of Joseph Nasi), pp. 42–3.

[22] The information is given in Hans Dernschwam's *Tagebuch*, more than once referred to above. It is possible, however, that he was thinking about her brother-in-law, Diogo, rather than her husband.

[23] See the chapter on the Tiberias Experiment in the life of Joseph Nasi which will appear as a sequel to this work.

[24] The passage is at the end of the report published by M.Stern, *Urkundliche Beiträge über die Stellung der Päpste zu den Juden*, pp. 138–143. Apparently there is a confusion of name between Gracia and her sister, unless Brianda is a variant of Beatrice. That the daughter was to marry the son of the sultan's physician had been bruited in Italy long before (see above, pages 56–7, 80), but it did not actually happen.

Notes to Chapter VI

[1] It is not easy to see what he means; the editor of this passage suggests the notorious Barbara of Cilli (Celje), consort of the Emperor Sigismund, who died in 1451, but this was hardly the way to speak of

an empress in those days. Perhaps the reference is to some notorious contemporary.

² It almost seems as though, like her nephews, she enjoyed some sort of official rank, to which this title alludes: for in the Hebrew sources she is referred to repeatedly as הגבירה המעטירה, which in the Hebrew of that day was intended to mean "the crowned" or "crowning lady" (cf. Isaiah 23.8) with a consistency which seems to suggest something more than conventional hyperbole.

³ Lungo, *Seder Zemanim*, pp. 42a–47a. It may be, however, that this passage is inspired by the encomium in Usque's *Consolaçam* (see above, page 77) rather than by Doña Gracia's activities while in Turkey.

⁴ Responsa, § xii.

⁵ Among the Portuguese Marranos whom she supported we know of Geronimo Dias, son of Manuel Alvares, who returned to Judaism under the name of Samuel Trogas and died in her house in Constantinople, the inheritance of his estate causing some perplexity to the local rabbis (Responsa of Joseph ibn Leb, III, 25).

⁶ ק"ק נרוש ספרד [קאשטילא] or ק"ק נרוש.

⁷ Responsa of Samuel de Medina, II, xcix.

⁸ A. Galante, *Histoire des Juifs d'Istanbul*, I, 123.

⁹ These — some thirty-six or more when Salonica was at its prime — continued to exist for the most part even after the disastrous fire of 1917, and down to the German occupation of 1941. The deportations which then followed reduced the community from some 56,000 (as against 80,000 a generation before) to fewer than 2,000, and at the same time almost all the Jewish institutions were uprooted. When I visited Salonica on behalf of the British army authorities in the summer of 1946 only two or three of the former synagogues were standing, only one was functioning and the Sabbath morning attendance did not exceed a couple of dozen. The martyrdom and quasi-obliteration of Salonican Jewry is one of the most appalling episodes of even our generation.

¹⁰ See his collection of sermons, *Maamez Koaeh* (Venice, 1588), § xxii; Moses Almosnino (about whom monographs have been written in French by Carmoly and in Hebrew by Molho and Ben-Menahem) figures also below, p. 183, and in various connections also in the sequel to this volume, on the Duke of Naxos.

¹¹ This is the normal Sephardi form; the Ashkenazi equivalent is *Bet Midrash*.

¹² Responsa of Samuel de Medina, IV, § 266.

¹³ There will be a chapter devoted to this fascinating episode in my biography of the Duke of Naxos.

Notes to Chapter VII

[1] Cf. the reference in the responsa of Isaac Lattes, p. 25.

[2] There is a detailed account of this in my *History of the Jews in Italy*, chapter VII, to which the reader is referred for fuller details.

[3] The form "Galnaba," frequently found in accounts of this episode, is the result of a misprint in the later editions of the Hebrew chronicle, *Shalshelet ha-Kabbalah*.

[4] This is made clear from more than one of the accounts: that the Ancona martyrs were burned alive is not correct.

[5] Amatus mentions, in his writings, his brother, Joseph Lusitanus (i. e. "Portuguese"), apparently living in Ancona; and I have before conjectured that the original family name was *Oheb* rather than *Habib*, as was formerly asserted without definite evidence. In some of the sources the person here in question is called Joseph Guascon. But "Joseph Habib, the martyr of Ancona" is referred to in the responsa of Samuel de Medina, IV, ccclxxx: his widow (like Amatus) had found refuge in Salonica.

[6] Following an earlier writer, I formerly identified the suicide with Doña Gracia's agent, Jacob Mosso, but a re-examination of the sources has made me question this. It is, however, noteworthy that a document in the Bodleian Library, Oxford (cf. Neubauer's *Catalogue*, § 2,000) refers to him by the unusual epithet (especially as applied to another) *he-Alub* ("the Miserable"), which would seem to support the hypothesis.

This would explain the discrepancy in the number of the victims in the various accounts, some lists possibly omitting the suicide from the roll of martyrs and some including him.

[7] The most interesting of these are conveniently republished in Bernfeld, *Sepher ha-Demaoth*, II, 320–350: cf. also the *Revue des Etudes Juives*, vols. XI, XXXI and LXXXIX. All the sources are listed in Steinschneider, *Geschichtsliteratur der Juden*, § 117.

There is in my own collection an old translation of Jacob da Fano's elegy in Italian *terza rima* (written in Hebrew characters) which adds a few details not in the original. I have corrected the names &c. in accordance with this. The ninth name is clearly given more than once as Finto, not Pinto.

[8] C. Garibaldi, *Un asserto Autodafé sotto Paolo IV* (Bologna, 1876).

[9a-b] This seems the simplest way to reconcile the divergent figures. With the twenty-six, there was one woman.

[10] This was the garment known in Spain and Portugal as the *sambenito*.

[11] He ultimately met his death by violence.

[12] Cf. the responsa of Samuel de Medina, IV, § § liv, lv, ccclxxx, lv; of Joseph ibn Leb, II, liv; of Isaac Adarbi, § 83.

[13] The words of Joseph ha-Cohen, in his *Emek ha-Bakha* (Valley of Tears"), p. 134, deserve quotation: —

And there was in Constantinople a certain great woman of the stock of the Marranos, whose name was Beatrice. She now went to the sultan and supplicated him; and he sent to Paul, the man of Belial, saying, "Send away my men": and the latter obeyed him. Yet this evil Theatine poured forth the vials of his anger upon the Marranos who were dwelling in Ancona, and there were burned of them twenty-four men and one old woman . . . and they cried as their soul went forth: "Hear, O Israel, the Lord our God is One God"; and their pure souls went up in the flame to heaven. Those who remained he turned away from the Lord, and he took all their property. There was never done in Italy an evil thing like this until now. Ye daughters of Israel, weep for these martyrs! Clothe you not in robes of silk, nor dress you in scarlet, for the glory is gone from Israel. My bowels go forth for those who are slain, and my soul refuseth comfort for those who are turned away. See Thou, O God, and behold and fight Thou their battle."

[14] This letter, formerly unknown, was published by P. Giangiacomi in the *Corriere Adriatico*, 8, ii, 1929.

[15] The text of the letter as published reads *Odoardo* (the Italian form of Duarte = Edward) *e Agostino Ibrio* — perhaps a misreading for *iberi*, or *ebrei*.

[16] *Lettere di Principi* (Venice, 1581), I, 177–8. There is a curious point to be noted in connection with this. The editor, Girolamo Ruscelli, was a friend of Duarte Gomez (the Marrano poet and businessman, who was intimately concerned in these events), who contributed a poem to his anthology in honor of Juana of Aragon, published in 1565. Could it have been through him that the compiler received the text of this confidential state document which must have been known to his principals in Constantinople?

The Pope's reply was published by P. Grunebaum in *Revue des Etudes Juives*, XVIII, 142–6.

[16a] This is perhaps a reference to the fact that the House of Nasi — particularly Don Joseph — farmed the Turkish customs at this time. Apparently the House tried to stimulate interest in the affair by professing themselves unable to pay their treasury-dues, on the plea that their losses in Ancona had been so heavy.

[17] Joseph ha-Cohen's statement (above, n. 13) that the Pope complied with the sultan's request and sent away Doña Gracia's men, is therefore misleading. On the other hand, it would appear that her other agents at Ancona were not of Portuguese birth and therefore escaped with their lives. Possibly, the Abraham Mosso and Hayyim Cohen whom we find in the employment of the family later on are

identical with the Abraham Mus and Azim Cohen who were formerly in her service here.

[18] Rabbi Joshua Soncino had a son named Eleazar, and it is probable therefore that his father was the printer of the same name.

[19] Forty *aspri* (in Hebrew, *Lebanim* or "whites") at this time made up one ducat or piastre, which was then roughly equivalent to an American dollar in 1939 values (though with a far greater purchasing power). After Murad III, there were 50 *aspri* to the piastre, and ultimately as many as 120.

[20] The current historians do not concur with the sources on this point, stating only that the rabbi of the Ashkenazi community refused to sign and lost his allowance, not the sequel.

[21] In my account, I have made full use of this extraordinarily interesting document, in Joshua Soncino's responsa, *Nahala li-Jehoshua*, § § xxxix–xl, to which I owe the intimate details which would otherwise seem purely imaginary. Cf. also the responsa of Joseph Caro [and Moses di Trani], I, ccxxxvii.

[22] Cf. the reference in *Revue des Etudes Juives*, XI, 150.

Notes to Chapter VIII

[1] In Saadiah Lungo's elegy, in his *Seder Zemanim*, pp. 42a–47a, the work of Doña Gracia's sister too is apparently alluded to in flattering terms; but the author's language is so obscure that it is impossible to draw definite conclusions.

[2] For these negotiations, see Hammer, *Geschichte des Osmanischen Reiches*, III, 364; and *Studi in onore di Ugo Hirsch* (Ferrara, 1931), p. 28 (article by Silvio Magrini, one of the victims of the Nazi-Fascist terror in Italy).

[3] See above, page 173.

[4] The details of the case are given in very great detail in Joshua Soncino's responsa, *Nahala li-Jehoshua*, § xx; to repeat all the minutiae here would be wearisome, but they are epitomized by H. Zimmels, *Die Marranen in der rabbinischen Literatur* (Berlin, 1932), pp. 129–135.

[5] A full account of this will be given in the chapter on Joseph Nasi's Tiberias experiment in the sequel to this volume, *The Duke of Naxos*.

[6] It is impossible to be dogmatic about this. The last thing we hear about Doña Gracia (1565) is that she was expected in Palestine, and, although there is no actual record that she arrived, the possibility must not be ruled out. It is perhaps significant that in the extremely detailed vision of the Nasi family in the "Treatise on Dreams" by her admirer, Moses Almosnino, at the close of his *Regimiento de la Vida*,

which was published in 1564 (see *The Duke of Naxos*), Doña Gracia
does not figure; possibly she had by now left Turkey.

[7] In Almosnino's memorial sermon in commemoration of her former
opponent, Rabbi Joshua Soncino, delivered on 10th Sivan, 1569 (in
his collection of addresses, *Maamez Koah*, Venice, 1588, p. 64 ff.)

[8] The text of these two addresses, which he apparently preserved
with others about women in a special collection, has unfortunately
not been preserved. We know, however, that the former one was an
elaboration of the dictum of Rabbi Meir (T. B. Berakhot, 17a) em-
phasizing the glory of departing from the world with a good name.
Almosnino refers to this in his memorial sermon on Joshua Soncino in
1569, and to the other in his commemoration of Astruc ibn Sahal
in 1570/1 (*Maamez Koah*, pp. 64a, 134a).